Why Terrorists Quit

Why Terrorists Quit

The Disengagement of Indonesian Jihadists

Julie Chernov Hwang

Cornell University Press

Ithaca and London

First published 2018 by Cornell University Press

Printed in the United States of America

Library of Congress Cataloging-in-Publication Data

Names: Chernov-Hwang, Julie, author.
Title: Why terrorists quit : the disengagement of Indonesian jihadists / Julie Chernov Hwang.
Description: Ithaca : Cornell University Press, 2018. | Includes bibliographical references and index.
Identifiers: LCCN 2017035096 (print) | LCCN 2017035884 (ebook) | ISBN 9781501710834 (epub/mobi) | ISBN 9781501710841 (pdf) | ISBN 9781501710827 | ISBN 9781501710827 (cloth : alk. paper)
Subjects: LCSH: Terrorists—Indonesia—Psychology. | Terrorism—Indonesia—Psychological aspects. | Terrorism—Religious aspects—Islam. | Jihad.
Classification: LCC HV6433.I5 (ebook) | LCC HV6433.I5 C54 2018 (print) | DDC 363.32509598—dc23
LC record available at https://lccn.loc.gov/2017035096

Cornell University Press strives to use environmentally responsible suppliers and materials to the fullest extent possible in the publishing of its books. Such materials include vegetable-based, low-VOC inks and acid-free papers that are recycled, totally chlorine-free, or partly composed of nonwood fibers. For further information, visit our website at cornellpress.cornell.edu.

For Dae and Sophia
and the late Rizal Panggabean

Contents

Preface   *ix*

Timeline   *xix*

Introduction   *1*

1 The Rise, Decline, and Resurgence of
    Jemaah Islamiyah   *22*

2 Patterns of Disengagement   *48*

3 Anas   *79*

4 B.R.   *91*

5 Ali Imron   *106*

6 Ali Fauzi   *121*

7 Yuda   *133*

8 The Role of the State and Civil Society in
    Disengagement Initiatives   *140*

Conclusion   *167*

Notes   *185*

Glossary   *199*

Index   *203*

Preface

The van arrived at the prison in Ampana a little after 9 a.m. We had left Palu around 10 p.m. the previous night—I was accompanied by my coresearchers on the Poso conflict Paramadina University lecturer Ihsan Ali Fauzi and Gadjah Mada University lecturer Rizal Panggabean, and our guide, A.B., who was at least six months pregnant at the time. As we raced up the highway in the night, I made several valiant attempts at sleeping, but between the loud snores of my colleagues and my head smacking against the van's window each time I nodded off, I was at a loss. When we finally stopped at sunup, I tumbled out of the van and into a roadside restaurant, where the floor was lined with pillows for seats. I lay down on a set of three and slept.

When I awoke again, the sun had risen. The mists had burned off, and the Bay of Poso was clearly visible. We washed up, ate a breakfast of fish and rice, went over the interview questions again, and resumed our trek. At some point in the drive, "Yusuf," a long-haired jihadi from Tanah Runtuh, Jemaah Islamiyah's affiliate in Poso, fell in behind the van on his motorcycle. We had interviewed him on a prior trip. He wore the same T-shirt as the first time we met. It had large green letters that said, "Live as a Good Muslim or Die as a Marytr" in English. He shook my hand, which struck me as odd, since devout Muslims tend to avoid physical contact with women outside their immediate families. I began to wonder if he wore the shirt to send a message, which had been my original presumption, or if he just liked that particular T-shirt. I thought about asking why he had come, but then thought better of it. I figured he had wanted to see his friend. He would later inform me that he had decided to join our research team; we needed "a guard," he asserted, and he would be our guard.

In the six years that I had been conducting research on the disengagement of Indonesian jihadists, I had interviewed some fifty-five people who had left Jemaah Islamiyah (JI), Mujahidin KOMPAK, or one of their affiliates in Poso or had shifted from a violent to a nonviolent role within that movement. However, up to that point, I had not interviewed anyone who was still committed to the use of violence against civilians.

On that day, however, we were going to interview "Yuda," one of the most notorious of the Poso jihadists, a former musician in a local rock band who, with the massacre of more than a dozen family members by Christian militiamen in 2000, traded his gang of drug- and alcohol-fueled musicians for a jihad gang. I imagined Yuda to be at least six feet tall and strapping. It was said he was covered in tattoos. Given the magnitude of his crimes, I assumed he would look intimidating. When he came into the room, however, I found that he was about my height—five foot five, with crudely drawn tattoos on his arms and pockmarked skin. I should have known better. Over the years that I have conducted this research, I had my preexisting assumptions about what a "terrorist" should look like challenged repeatedly. When I started out, I imagined dead eyes, angry eyes. Instead, I met young men who looked as ordinary as the next person. Of the young men I had interviewed, no one had ever intimidated me or shaken me until that day. Yuda told us his story, how the loss of his family propelled him to seek revenge and why he remained committed to the use of violence.

On our way out, he turned to me and asked, "Will you kill President Obama for me?" I froze for a moment. I remember thinking, how did this become my life? How could I ever be in a situation where someone would ask me that question? How do I answer this question, get out the door, and remain safe? I turned to him, took a deep breath, and said as calmly as I could muster, "No. I do not kill." I thanked him for the interview, and we left. Later, while swimming in the Bay of Poso, I put the question to Yusuf, using the patois of our research group to make the point in a nonserious manner. "Hey, Yusuf, why is Yuda crazy, while you're just half crazy?" By this time, we had agreed that each of us in the research group was "half crazy," and we had been tossing the term around for the better part of the day. He answered, "Yuda does not mingle." I responded, "So you relaxed because you have mingled?" He said yes. It was that simple.

Of the research I've done in my academic career, nothing is more challenging or fascinating than disengagement. When I began this research, I thought I would write one article on the disengagement of jihadists in Poso with two colleagues and then return to the seemingly safer study of Islamist parties. What I did not realize at that time was that jihadists and ex-jihadists from Jemaah Islamiyah and their affiliates would talk with me and share their stories. In time, I began to see patterns emerging from these stories, which mirrored those found among former fighters from the Ulster Volunteer Forces, the Euskadi ta Askatasuna (ETA), and Scandinavian skinhead groups.

If we want to understand jihadists, we must talk to them. That requires working through guides and sitting down over coffee, tea, or a meal or visiting during prison visiting hours. Moreover, if one is going to attempt to truly understand a person, it is always best to go back more than once and attempt to build a relationship. This does not mean that the interviewer and interviewee become best friends. However, it does mean you attempt to empathize with the person and his or her narrative. This is what I've attempted to do over the course of this project.

The results of this project are based on nearly a decade of building good relations with trusted friends, who, about seven years ago, agreed to share their contacts in Islamist extremist communities with me, after coming to understand the focus and goals of this project. One was an academic, one was a journalist, two were human rights activists, and two worked for a noted terrorist rehabilitation NGO. From their own research or their own work, each had built a network of contacts within the Indonesian jihadist community. Each of these guides introduced me to a number of current and former JI, Mujahidin KOMPAK, Ring Banten, Tanah Runtuh, or Mujahidin Kayamanya members who were open to speaking with me, a non-Muslim American woman, and to sharing their stories with me. In my research in Central Sulawesi, I conducted interviews in Poso, Palu, and Ampana in conjunction with two counterparts, Ihsan Ali Fauzi and Rizal Panggabean.

I do not doubt that some of those I interviewed obfuscated, left out information, or outright lied to me. However, since thirty people highlighted the same four points in their disengagement narratives, it is unlikely that they *all* coordinated with one another across two islands and six provinces. Some of them had to trust me or at least came to trust me over repeated visits. One way I attempted to cultivate that trust was being very honest about my motivations. I felt that the subject of disengagement had been given short shrift. People wanted to know about how jihadis were radicalized and what they did. However, the idea that someone could leave an Islamist extremist group or reintegrate into society and the motives as to why were insufficiently explored. I sought to humanize them via telling their stories to people outside their communities, to people in the West and in Indonesia. To be clear, this book does not attempt to condone the actions of the jihadists I interviewed. However, if we are going to understand why individuals would participate directly or indirectly in a terrorist attack, or join a jihad and participate in an act of terror in the context of a jihad, we must find a way to attempt to empathize and, in so doing, understand their motives, even though we disagree with their choices.

It was also important to protect their rights and to respect their privacy. Individuals approached to be interviewed had three opportunities for refusal. They could refuse when they were initially contacted by the guide. They could refuse again when we sought confirmation closer to the date. They could also refuse by not showing up for the interview or by going quiet and cold at the interview. However, in most instances, those contacted accepted the interview. As often as possible, I sought to interview the same person multiple times over repeated visits over the six years I was conducting this research.

At the start of the interview, I explained who I was; the nature and the goals of the project; and the ethics and obligations of the researcher. I stated that I had a duty to protect their identity to the best of my ability and that they were under no obligation to answer a question that made them uncomfortable. I sought permission both to use an audio recording device and to quote them. I asked them if they wished me to use a specially constructed alias for this project or a generic title. In most cases, I was using their interviews to support the broad-patterns data and told them as much. In instances where I wrote life histories or shared a substantial portion of their narrative, I went back to those individuals and asked permission to tell their life history. If they consented, I asked them to choose a name by which I would refer to them. All the subjects of life histories, with the exception of Yuda, were interviewed three to five times between 2010 and 2016. This has given me the opportunity to see them build new lives, go back to school, obtain master's degrees, get out of jail, start new businesses, marry and have children. (Yuda escaped from prison in 2013 and fled into the mountains to join the East Indonesia Holy Warriors; I had no intention to try to find him.) As often as possible with the life histories, I have met spouses, siblings, parents, and children. This offers a unique opportunity to truly unpack disengagement and understand the process.

When interviews were conducted in prisons, my guides first sought permission from the jihadist himself. Upon obtaining that permission, they then sought permission from the relevant authorities in the Department of Corrections and then in the prison itself. Closer to the date, interviews were reconfirmed with the jihadist, who was told that his participation in any interview was voluntary. I received permission from the Goucher College Institutional Review Board to conduct these interviews, as well as the interviews outside prison. We agreed that I would use general titles or pseudonyms, that prisoners would be apprised orally of their rights and the risks of participation, and that they would be told that we could stop or skip questions at any time. Interviews in prisons were conducted in public areas like a garden, an open indoor or outdoor visiting room, or, on one occasion, in the cell itself. Prison officials were not permitted to sit in on the interview. When Ali Imron insisted that I write his life history under his own name, we agreed—after I had consulted with the

Goucher review board—that he would write a letter to the board explaining that he understood the risks of doing so and accepted those risks.

Non-prison interviews (the majority of all interviews) were conducted in neutral locations, including cafés, a guide's home, or the office of a community group. Whenever possible, I supplemented interview data with autobiographies, biographies, and draft monographs of the militants themselves, public interviews, and court proceedings.

Those I interviewed were certainly a self-selecting group, which does bias the research outcome to a certain extent. This cannot be avoided. However, I did my best to maximize the variation in cause of radicalization, level of involvement, region, group, and degree of disengagement. Research with clandestine groups cannot often be as scientific as survey research or polling. Yet I contend that the findings of this study indicate that strong patterns exist, and that from those patterns we can highlight the factors that are the greater predictors of successful disengagement and subsequently reintegration.

Acknowledgments

I would first like to thank the *ikhwan* from Jemaah Islamiyah, Mujahidin KOMPAK, Ring Banten, Tanah Runtuh, Mujahidin Kayamanya, and Laskar Jihad who shared their stories with me. Anas, B.R., Ali Imron, Ali Fauzi, Agus, Reza, and Yuda, thank you for allowing me to write your life histories so that others can understand your perspectives, narratives, and journeys. Anas and B.R., thank you especially for introducing me to your families. It was enlightening to learn their perspectives on your journeys. Thank you for that trust.

This work would not have been possible without the assistance of Noor Huda Ismail, Taufik Andrie, Badrus Sholeh, Adriany, Yono, and Farouk, who opened up their networks of contacts, facilitated meetings, secured consent, accompanied me to meetings, and shared not only their perspectives, and their work with me but also their genuine friendship. Rizal Panggabean and Ihsan Ali Fauzi accompanied me on many a visit to Palu and Poso. I became a far better interviewer working alongside these two scholars. Many thanks also to Zora Sukabdi, Dharmawan Ronodipuro, and Agus Hadi Nagrahoui for sharing their perspective on rehabilitation programs, alongside Noor Huda, Taufik, and the team at the Institute for International Peacebuilding (YPP).

This research was funded by a series of summer research grants from Goucher College and a 2011 US-Indonesia Society Travel Grant. Chapter 3 was written when I was a visiting Southeast Asia fellow at the East-West Center in Washington, DC. The EWC, the US-Indonesia Society, the Indonesia program at the Rajaratnam School for International Studies, Johns Hopkins SAIS, the Indonesia Studies Group at Australian National University, the Center for Middle East Studies and Global Peace at the State Islamic University–Syarif Hidayatullah, and the Faculty of Islamic Studies at Universitas Islam 45 Bekasi and Universitas Penelitian Harapan provided venues in which to showcase the results of this research over the years in its various incarnations. In this regard, specific thanks go to Satu Limaye, David Merrill, Bill Wise, Leonard Sebastian, Alex Arifianto, Kumar Ramakrisna, Purnama Putra, and Yosef Djakababa. Thank you.

I am so lucky to have been in such good hands as Cornell University Press. Roger Malcolm Haydon has been a tremendous editor, offering advice at every stage for how to improve the book in order to increase the appeal of this project to a wider readership.

Many thanks also to Meagan Dermody, Ange Romeo-Hall, Glenn Novak, Richanna Patrick, and Martyn Beeny and the entire marketing team. You are all exceptional at what you do.

I am grateful to Marc Roy, Goucher's former provost, for believing in the project and ensuring that, either through the provost's office or via the official grant itself, I could continue this research. Many thanks to our current provost, Leslie Lewis, for her support as well. I also want to thank my colleagues on Goucher's Institutional Review Board—Dara, Carolyn, Rory, Janet, Phyllis, Ann Marie, and Jennifer. It may have taken us months to work through the ethics and the language, but you helped me to keep the ethics of this research at the forefront of my mind. Barbara Stob, thank you for your attention to the legal angles as well. You were the angels on my shoulder.

A great many colleagues have offered input on draft chapters and shared their perspective on the book's organization, structure, argument, methods, and the institutional review board (IRB) process. I am deeply grateful to John Horgan for his advice at various junctures of this project on subject matter as varied as how to conduct psychological interviews, to how to navigate the IRB, to the importance of a methodological preface. Mia Bloom, thank you for your gracious advice regarding the IRB, and T Kumar, thank you for offering your insights to Goucher's IRB. Sidney Jones and Greg Fealy, you are truly generous souls. Bill Liddle, thank you for being a source of constant encouragement. Ronit Berger, Bozena Welborne, and Bill Safran, I appreciate your taking the time to offer such detailed feedback for rewriting chapter 1 for a nonspecialist audience. Much gratitude also to Kirsten Schulze, Navhat Nuraniyah, Joseph Liow, A'an Suryana, Yosef Djakababa, Adnuri Mohaimidi, Solahudin, Omar Ashour, Sulastri Osman, Bill Finan, Lawrence Rubin, Endy Bayuni, Jennifer Munger, Thomas

Hegghammer, Jillian Schwedler, Mark Woodward, Ray Hervadi, Tom Pepinsky, and Greg Barton, and the two anonymous reviewers. Nelly Lahoud, thank you so much for being a sounding board on the argument. It has never been the same since you left Goucher; you are truly missed.

Dae, thank you for believing in me and for trusting that I knew what I was doing. Sophia, your mother loves learning via fieldwork. You'll realize this soon enough. Thank you for being the reason I love coming home. Thank you both for being the light.

Timeline

1949–62	Darul Islam wages rebellions against the Indonesian government in West Java, Aceh, and South Sulawesi.
1962	Darul Islam's Aceh and West Java rebellions end. Kartosuwirjo, the leader of the West Java rebellion, is arrested and executed.
1971	BAKIN funds a Darul Islam reunion.
1973	Darul Islam chooses a new leadership.
1976–77	Darul Islam's Medan branch launches a series of terror attacks under the leadership of Gaos Taufik. Warman, "the *fai* king," and his associates embark on a *fai* campaign—robbing "unbelievers" to pay for jihad.
1976	Abdullah Sungkar and Abu Bakar Ba'asyir, the founders of Jemaah Islamiyah, join Darul Islam.
1980	Darul Islam becomes an underground organization.
1985	Abdullah Sungkar and Abu Bakar Ba'asyir flee to Malaysia rather than face imprisonment.

1985–91   Abdullah Sungkar and Abu Bakar Ba'asyir become the conduit for Indonesians who want to fight in the Soviet-Afghan War.

1993   Abdullah Sungkar and Abu Bakar Ba'asyir break from Darul Islam and form Jemaah Islamiyah.

1996   Jemaah Islamiyah authors its General Guidelines of Struggle articulating its goals, the process of attaining those goals, and its organizational structure.

1998   The thirty-two-year dictatorship of Suharto and the New Order falls.

1998   Osama bin Laden issues a fatwa calling on Muslims to kill Americans and their allies.

1998   Communal violence breaks out in Poso.

1999   Communal violence breaks out in Ambon.

1999   KOMPAK sends humanitarian relief to Ambon. JI members travel via KOMPAK. KOMPAK and JI join in the fighting.

2000   Mujahidin KOMPAK and then JI arrive in Poso following the May 2000 Walisongo massacre.

2001   The Malino declaration attempts to establish peace in Poso. Small-scale terror attacks continue until 2007.

2002   The Malino II declaration attempts to establish peace in Ambon. Small-scale violence continues.

2000–2001   At Hambali's urging, Imam Samudra forms a team to carry out bombings against Christian targets. They carry out the Medan bombing, the

	Christmas Eve bombing, and attempt to bomb a church in the Atrium Mall.
2002	Imam Samudra and Muchlas mastermind the first Bali bombing.
2003	Noordin M. Top and Dr. Azhari Husin mastermind the JW Marriott bombing.
2003–6	Small-scale terror attacks take place in Poso.
2004	Noordin M. Top and Dr. Azhari Husin mastermind the Australian Embassy bombing.
2005	Break between JI leadership and Noordin M. Top's faction—al Qaeda in the Malay Archipelago.
2005	Noordin M. Top and Dr. Azhari Husin mastermind the second Bali bombing.
2009	Noordin M. Top and Dr. Azhari Husin mastermind the Marriott and Ritz-Carlton bombings.
2010	Lintas Tanzim initiative tries and fails to create a secure base in Aceh.
2012	HASI starts trips to Syria.
2016	ISIS affiliates bomb Jakarta Starbucks.

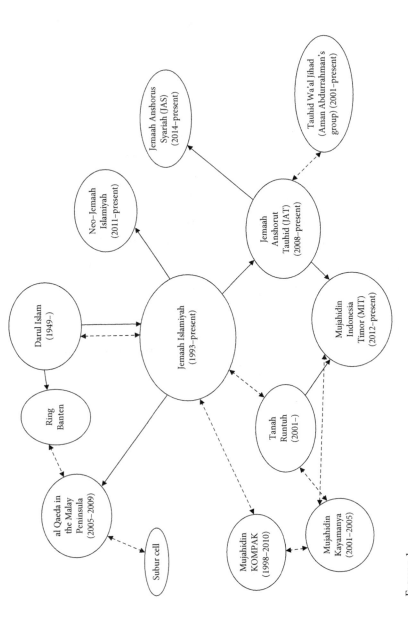

FIGURE 1

Jemaah Islamiyah and its affiliates. Dotted lines denote affiliation; solid lines denote splinters.

Why Terrorists Quit

Introduction

A Jemaah Islamiyah member goes into a church to leave a bomb. Once inside, he stays for the service. After the bombing, he begins to feel guilty. These Christians had not attacked Muslims, as the Christian paramilitaries in Ambon city had. These Christians knew nothing. If his group was going to mount an attack, why not attack the central authorities in Ambon? In time, he pushes those feelings out of his mind. He subsequently participates in the bombing of the Philippine ambassador's residence and the first Bali bombing, his roles growing more indirect each time and his emotional response increasingly disconnected.

In the aftermath of the Bali bombing, however, where his role was confined to driving the car from Java to Bali, he went on the run with Ali Imron. Hiding out in Kalimantan, they began to discuss the bombings. These conversations continued after their imprisonment. They came to the conclusion that the Bali bombing had been wrong because innocent civilians were targeted. Suryadharma, then the head of Densus 88, the police counterterror team, also helped him to broaden his perspective, for he took him and other imprisoned jihadis on field trips to orphanages or to visit scavengers to show the prisoners how they could help the

Muslim community in a nonviolent manner. The combination of his guilty feelings over his role in the attacks, the rational assessment that he and Ali Imron did together, the solidarity fostered by their friendship and the fact they held the same position on the use of violence, and the influence of Suryadharma persuaded him to psychologically disengage.

While numerous studies describe the goals, methods, and motives of a particular terrorist group, attempt to identify the root causes of terrorism, examine specific methods used by terrorist groups, such as suicide bombings, or highlight the process of radicalization of terrorists or militants, far fewer highlight why a militant would chose to turn away from terror tactics and terror groups.[1] However, terrorist campaigns do end, radical groups demobilize and disarm, and individuals do disengage from violence.

A movement may use terror tactics at a certain point in its life cycle and subsequently choose to abandon those tactics. The leadership of al Gamaah al Islamiyah, formerly a founding affiliate of al Qaeda, abandoned the use of violence in 1997 in response to new opportunities for interaction; concerns among the leadership about increased exposure to those jihadists who were willing to pronounce *takfir* (excommunication) without just cause;[2] selective inducements; and state repression.[3] Occurring over the next decade, the process of revision, a textually grounded systematic reassessment of previously held beliefs, resulted in the publication of some twenty-seven books and pamphlets detailing al Gamaah al Islamiyah's new system of thought. This was accompanied on the government's part by the release from prison of some twenty thousand of the organization's members.[4] In January 2011, al Gamaah al Islamiyah formed a political party, Hizb al-Banna' wa al-Tanmiyya (the Building and Development Party) and contested the 2011–12 elections as part of the Islamist Alliance, together with the Salafist An Nour party and others.

In Indonesia, Laskar Jihad, the paramilitary wing of the Ahl Sunna Communication Forum (FKAWJ), disarmed and demobilized following the 2002 Bali bombings in response to internal accusations that the group's leaders and the group itself had been moving away from its raison d'être (defending Muslims) and injecting itself too much in politics. According to the group's former spokesman, Hardi Ibnu Harun,

> Laskar Jihad was [participating in] demonstrations, clashes with other groups, clashes with the government, and police officers. This is not appropriate. There was the case in Ngawi [where] friends were arrested for fighting with the police. There were many other cases in other areas where Laskar Jihad deviated from the values of our teachers.[5]

To support this decision, leaders sought a fatwa on the issue from one of their Middle Eastern "teachers," Rabi ibn Hadi al-Madkhali, a Saudi Arabian imam. Their leaders socialized the decision through meetings and via the Internet. Over the course of several months, the Salafi paramilitary group turned over its weapons to authorities, and members went back to their Islamic schools on Java.

Terrorist groups, however, may lack the leadership and organizational structure necessary to implement a decision to abandon violence among their membership and keep them unified in doing so. In those cases, disengagement may occur on an individual level or on a factional level as certain leaders and members come to the conclusion that violence is counterproductive, while others form violent splinter factions. This type of disengagement has occurred among Jemaah Islamiyah members in Indonesia, Malaysia, and Singapore.[6]

To examine the processes and pathways through which individuals disengage from violence, we need to first answer three interrelated questions. What is disengagement? What factors lead militants to disengage from violence? To what extent is disengagement subject to internal or external incentives?

Unpacking Disengagement

Disengagement is a process through which a member of a terrorist group, radical movement, gang, or cult chooses to cease participation in acts of violence, either via leaving the movement or by migrating from a violent to a nonviolent role in the movement. The term connotes a change in behavior, in contrast to ideological deradicalization, which denotes the delegitimation of the ideology underpinning the use of violence.[7] In other words, deradicalization refers to a change in values and attitudes.[8] Within a terrorist group or radical movement, individual views of violence may vary significantly across factions and members, and those views may be quite nuanced. One may view specific types of attacks as permissible under certain conditions but not others. Thus, individuals may disengage (i.e., change their behavior) without completely deradicalizing (i.e., changing their core beliefs on the legitimacy of violence).[9]

Disengagement is a process. Each factor, relationship, and interaction builds on prior ones, as the individual assesses his or her views on violence, participation in acts of violence, the conditions under which that participation is permissible or not, and whether or not it is in that individual's interest to remain in the group.

Moreover, the disengagement process is gradual. No one wakes up one day and decides to leave a terror group or abandon violence. Instead, it is a process of months, even years of reflection, discussion, and consideration; of incremental steps that don't always go in the same direction; and dozens of small decisions. Adriana Faranda, a former member of the Italian Red Brigades, explains her "dissociation" from the Marxist group as

> a process which matured very gradually. . . . It's not a traumatic leap, it is more a matter of a thousand little stages. It encompasses everything though; reasoning, valuations, questions, which involve not just one action, not one way of conducting the armed struggle, not one revolutionary project—everything. It involves the revolution itself; Marxism, violence, the logic of enmity, of conflict, of one's relationship with authority, a way of working out problems, of confronting reality and of facing the future. . . . I haven't taken one huge traumatic leap. It's not as if I was one person one day and a different one the next.[10]

Another way of thinking about this process is in comparison to the initial radicalization trajectory. Just as radicalization is typically incremental in nature, with increasing tests of commitment and slow movement toward greater illegality, so too is the move away from violence a similarly gradual process.[11]

The disengagement process is also not necessarily linear or always forward moving. It may proceed in fits and starts. An individual may feel disillusioned with a specific terror act, for example, only to have those feelings ebb over time. Moreover, the building of new relationships takes time, and one's old in-group allegiances compete for influence with the new extra-group ones. Not everyone who feels guilt at a particular action or disillusionment with a colleague's or a superior's decision making will inevitably disengage. Instead, in-movement seniors, leaders, and friends may offer inducements to recommit to movement activities or participate in training, which can represent pathways back to radicalism. Additionally, should one maintain ties with the movement, even after disengagement, new opportunities for reengagement—for example, the opportunity to fight abroad in Syria or Iraq—may prove too tempting. As one's new relationships grow stronger and as one's priorities shift and one's investment in those priorities deepens, however, the commitment to disengagement becomes increasingly firm, and the individual may begin to reintegrate back into the broader society.

Furthermore, the decision to disengage does not necessitate a complete break with the group.[12] One can disengage by leaving the movement, going inactive; or by shifting from a violent to a nonviolent role in the movement.[13] It may be difficult for a member to break with the movement entirely, because of the positive affective bonds and benefits gained from membership, most notably family ties, marital ties, discipleship, a sense of extended kinship due to long-standing friendships, and a common sense of identity.[14] Others may disagree with specific violent tactics like bombings but remain believers in the overall goal and be working in small capacities toward its realization. Still others may go inactive but retain friends in the group. Even those who have left a movement entirely may see benefits to remaining on the fringes. "Amru," for example, a former member of Jemaah Islamiyah, explained that while he no longer considered himself a member of JI, he still sends his children to a JI-affiliated school.

> It's a good school. They separate boys and girls. Muhammadiyah schools don't do that. Nahdlatul Ulama schools don't do that. If there were a Salafi school of the same quality, I would send my children there.[15]

Yet this ensures that Amru sees other members of Jemaah Islamiyah on at least a daily basis, at the drop-off and pickup of his children.

Disengagement can often be viewed as conditional, especially if one's radicalization trajectory occurred under specific conditions, such as the outbreak of communal conflict. In experiencing the reflective process of disengagement, individuals may question the conditions under which they would reengage. The important point is not whether a condition exists but *what* the condition is. Individuals who revise their understanding of jihad from offensive *and* defensive to exclusively defensive and who decide that they would take up arms again only if their country was invaded have made a dramatic shift in their thinking. The likelihood they would reengage again is exceedingly slim. Individuals who were radicalized via communal conflict and who decide they would take up arms again if facing an invasion by the opposing force may be dealing in the realm of what they see as pragmatic. Someone who would like to join a foreign jihad but is not making an effort to find the funds may be in a similar position. The importance is not whether the condition exists but whether the bar is set so high as to preclude the realistic possibility of further involvement, or set sufficiently low that one may reengage under the right circumstances.

In some instances, a person who disengages from violence may also seek to reintegrate into society. This will most likely occur in those cases where someone goes inactive or leaves an extremist group. Reintegration, like disengagement, is also a process. One reintegrates into society by building an alternative social identity that competes for loyalty and may eventually displace one's identity as an extremist. A person finds a job, makes new friends, and eventually these relationships and priorities take precedence over the old ones. It is important to note that there is considerable overlap between the factors that encourage disengagement and re-integration. It would be useful for academic purposes if we could say that certain factors facilitate disengagement while others assist with reintegration, but this would be a false dichotomy. The same factors function differently at different points in the disengagement and reintegration processes.

Why Militants Disengage

This book examines the disengagement narratives of fifty-five jihadis from seven Indonesian Islamist extremist groups. It will argue that disengagement is driven by a combination of psychological, emotional, relational, and strategic factors. Often, one factor sparks reflection, and, in time, other factors interact with prior ones, pushing the individual further along the pathway to disengagement and, in some cases, toward reintegration into the broader society. From the interviews, this book identifies four factors that play key roles in the disengagement process: (1) disillusionment with the group's tactics and leaders; (2) rational assessment, where one comes to analyze the extent to which the context has changed or whether the costs of continued actions outweigh potential benefits; (3) the establishment of an alternative social network of friends, mentors, and sympathetic family members; and (4) a shift in priorities toward gainful employment and family life.

When I first started out, I assumed all four factors held the same weight. Yet, over repeated interviews, I learned that disillusionment and rational assessment rarely led to disengagement on their own, because loyalty to the group would often trump disillusionment and cost-benefit analysis in the absence of interaction with other factors. Disillusionment and rational assessment, taken together, strengthened each other but still did not get someone from disengagement to reintegration. Individuals might disengage, but they would remain in the movement, interacting primarily with individuals from the movement.

The linchpin of successful disengagement and subsequent re-integration was the interaction between building of an alternative social network composed of supportive friends, family members, and mentors and the shift in priorities toward job, family, and fur-thering one's education. Relationships could facilitate or reinforce priority shifts. They offered alternative narratives for understand-ing the "enemy"; an opportunity to reassess previously held views in light of new information; a support structure; critical assistance in formulating a post-jihad identity; and incentives for ongoing commitment to that identity. By contrast, recidivists were found to lack alternative social networks. This was true even in cases where their narratives included feelings of disillusionment.

Theories of Disengagement

The issue of why terrorism ends has been examined cross-nationally, at the group level and at the individual level, by just a handful of scholars. Scholars to date have been far more inter-ested in why people join terror movements than why they leave. The various streams of research within the terrorism literature have tended to focus instead on profiles of specific groups that detail their organization, structure, and tactics; analyses of spe-cific events; assessments of the organizational dynamics and be-havior of terror groups; and broad studies detailing the causes of terrorism or the types of terror groups in operation.[16] Moreover, since 9/11, there has been a veritable outpouring of research on al Qaeda, examining various aspects of the network, including its ideology, its primary texts, its methods, and its preparations for terror actions, with research varying from the robust to the polemical.[17] We have seen a similar flood of research with the rise of ISIS.[18] Understanding the process of turning away from terrorism, however, is critical to effective counterterrorism strategy and to understanding terrorist motivations more broadly.

In a robust comparative historical analysis, Audrey Kurth Cronin identifies six factors that have contributed to the end of terror campaigns: the capture and killing of a group's leader; the group's decision to enter formal politics; achievement of group objectives; alienation of the mass public; repression; and the transition from terrorism to other forms of violence.[19] She notes how several of these factors may interact with one another, and as a result, dynamics internal to the group may create conditions conducive to the group's demise, while state behavior via repression, negotiation, or facilitating political transition may reinforce the shift.[20]

In his analysis of organizational disengagement[21] (or what he refers to as organizational deradicalization) in Egypt and Algeria, Omar Ashour finds that when a movement possesses charismatic leadership, it is better able to react to state inducements to disengage or deradicalize and may be more willing and able to engage with individuals from outside the jihadi circle who offer alternative perspectives.[22] Moreover, the leaders are better able to compel their members to obey the decision. As a consequence, they are more likely to reconsider the use of violence, disarm, and reevaluate the ideological underpinnings of that violence.[23] Additionally, the presence of such charismatic leaders makes it less likely the movement will split as a result of its demobilization.[24]

But what happens if a movement lacks such charismatic leaders? What if a terror group is so fragmented that the campaign may change but ultimately does not end, and disengagement occurs among individuals and factions rather than movement-wide?

There is a growing literature on individual-level disengagement that analyzes the pathways to and processes of disengagement of ex-militants on the extreme right, the communist left, Irish and Basque nationalist movements, and, to a lesser degree, religious terror movements and pirates.[25]

Through interviews with members of Irish nationalist and radical Islamist terror movements, John Horgan has developed a typology of disengagement based on individual behavior, which examines the processes through which individuals become radicalized and then disengage from violent movements.[26] Horgan distinguishes two types of disengagement: physical and psychological. An individual physically disengages by migrating from a violent to a nonviolent role within the group, leaving it altogether, dying, or being expelled from the movement.[27] An individual disengages psychologically from violence because of disillusionment over tactics, strategy, ideology; an inability to reconcile the disconnect between the fantasy and reality of being involved in a terrorist group; burnout; or changing priorities.[28]

Tore Bjørgo, a criminologist specializing in Scandinavian neo-Nazi and far-right extremist movements, operationalizes the disengagement process based on a series of factors that may "push" the extremist away from the violent movement or "pull" them toward a "normal" life.[29] Notable push factors include the sense that "things have gone too far"; disillusionment with the inner workings of the group; negative social sanctions from family or community; and a loss of faith in the movement. Pull factors include the desire for gainful employment and family.[30] One especially notable pull factor that emerges is fatherhood, which can prompt reprioritization by militants, especially among those who already feel disillusioned by the tactics and leaders of a movement.[31] Fernando Reinares, a scholar examining the Euskadi ta Askatasuna (ETA), highlights the role of changing political context in disengagement, noting that after Basques had won regional autonomy, some fighters felt "it just didn't make sense anymore."[32] Renee Garfinkel adds that friends and mentors can assist in fostering commitment to the peaceful path.[33] The concept of push and pull factors is quite useful in understanding what specifically causes one to disengage and reintegrate.

While the literature on individual-level disengagement may have been built atop primarily European cases, including the Provisional Irish Republican Army, the Italian Red Brigades, ETA, and Scandinavian gangs, interviews conducted for this book found that jihadis are indeed disengaging from violence in response to many of the same incentives and drivers that are found among their militant counterparts in Europe.[34] This may indicate that, when it comes to disengagement, there are similarities between a religiously motivated militant and one motivated by nationalist or Marxist means. Relationships, disillusionment, context, and priority shifts are key drivers across individuals, irrespective of group, ideology, or region.

Much of the literature on deradicalization and disengagement in the Muslim world is composed of evaluative studies, which assess the strengths and weaknesses of the Saudi, Yemeni, Singaporean, Egyptian, Malaysian, or Indonesian programs.[35] Horgan and Altier note that a common factor among all such programs is an effort to change views that legitimate the use of violence.[36] Some of these programs, notably the Saudi and Singaporean programs, take it a step further, seeking to wholly reeducate offending terrorists away from their current jihadi-Salafi interpretation of Islam toward a version of Islam that is more acceptable to the state.[37] One approach favored in discussions of reintegration focuses not on reprogramming but instead on "reducing idleness" via job training and professional development.[38] Samuel Mullins notes that ex-terrorists typically need assistance in "establishing a legitimate life" if they are to successfully reintegrate.[39] The Danish program for ISIS returnees follows this train of thought; those eligible receive help in obtaining employment, housing, and educational assistance.[40] Similarly, the Singaporeans and Saudis also offer aftercare assistance to newly released participants in their programs.[41] Even small-scale reintegration programs can be useful in preventing recidivism, if they are well targeted and well planned.[42] If the programs are not developed with an understanding of the needs of the target population, however, they are likely to fall short.[43]

Why Disengagement in Indonesia?

If one wants to understand the disengagement of jihadists, there is perhaps no better place to look than Indonesia. With a population of 255 million people, 87 percent of whom are Muslim, Indonesia is the largest Muslim nation in the world and among the world's few Muslim democracies. To put those numbers in perspective, its total Muslim population exceeds that of Pakistan (181 million), Afghanistan (32.6 million), and Saudi Arabia (27.7 million) combined. Indonesia has had free and fair elections since transitioning to democracy in 1999, and freedom of association, press, and expression are respected by the state. As a result, Islamists can advocate for an Islamic state and Islamic law via the press, demonstrations, and through the political system without fear of repression or other negative repercussions. Sidney Jones notes that Indonesia's stable, democratic character and tolerance for those working for Islamic law have reduced the pull of extremist groups like ISIS.[44]

Indonesia has long had an Islamist extremist fringe, dating back to the Darul Islam rebellions of the independence era. The landscape of this fringe has been notable for its tendencies toward fragmentation, with groups splintering over issues of ideology, personality, and, importantly, when, where, and under what conditions violence is permissible. In January 1993, Darul Islam leaders Abdullah Sungkar and Abu Bakar Ba'asyir split from Darul Islam proper and established Jemaah Islamiyah, a group composed partly of Indonesian Afghan veterans with a goal of establishing an Islamic state in Indonesia. A faction within Jemaah Islamiyah carried out a series of terrorist attacks between 2000 and 2003, including the bombings of eleven churches on Christmas Eve 2000 resulting in 19 dead and approximately 100 injured; the attempted bombing of a church inside the Atrium Mall in 2001; the 2002 Bali bombing that killed some 202 people; and the bombing of the JW Marriott Hotel that killed 12 and injured 150 in 2003. That faction would later splinter off and form its own independent hyper-violent cell, al Qaeda in the Malay Archipelago. However, JI was not the only violent Islamist extremist organization during this period.[45] After the fall of the thirty-two-year New Order regime in 1998, Darul Islam emerged from underground and fragmented into nine separate factions, some of which were violent. Other radical Islamists established new groups, including Mujahidin KOMPAK and Laskar Jundullah. Communal conflicts in Ambon and Poso birthed several local Islamist extremist paramilitaries, including Tanah Runtuh, Mujahidin Kayamanya, and later, Mujahidin Indonesia Timur. In 2008, JI would further factionalize when JI cofounder Abu Bakar Ba'asyir left the movement and established Jemaah Anshorut Tauhid as a partially aboveground, partially clandestine movement. Today, Indonesian Islamist extremist groups are divided between those whose leadership have sworn loyalty to ISIS (Jemaah Anshorut Tauhid, Mujahidin Indonesia Timur, Ring Banten, Tauhid Wa'al Jihad) and those who are anti-ISIS (Jemaah Islamiyah and Jemaah Anshorus Syariah).

The Indonesian Islamist extremist fringe offers rich opportunities for those seeking to understand why Indonesian jihadists are disengaging from violence. One can seek out patterns across movements, regions, roles, and generations. By maximizing this cross-group variation, we can have more confidence in the pathways and patterns identified. Also important: the fact that Indonesia is a democracy reduces the risk for those jihadists who consent to be interviewed.

Who Are the Jihadists?

Between 2010 and 2016, I conducted over one hundred interviews with fifty-five jihadists[46] across seven militant and jihadist groups (Jemaah Islamiyah, Mujahidin KOMPAK, Ring Banten, Tanah Runtuh, Mujahidin Kayamanya, the Subur cell, and Laskar Jihad) in eight Indonesian cities (Jakarta, Yogyakarta, Solo, Semarang, Surabaya, Poso, Palu, Ampana). While all the jihadists may have come from the same country, they differed significantly on a variety of measures, including the causes of radicalization, their backgrounds, their education levels and types, familial links to radical movements, whether they had participated in a terror attack, their role in the organization, and the manner in which they were disengaging, if they disengaged at all.

Among those interviewed, almost half (twenty-three) had been radicalized by local conflict, in all but one case by the outbreak of communal conflict in the Poso district. These young men had joined one of two Islamist extremist groups in Poso—Tanah Runtuh or Mujahidin Kayamanya—depending on where they lived.

Tanah Runtuh became Jemaah Islamiyah's affiliate in Poso. Mujahidin Kayamanya was affiliated with another Islamist extremist group from Java, Mujahidin KOMPAK. In a majority of cases, the catalyst for the young men's radicalization had been the 2000 Walisongo massacre, where over one hundred men, women, and children were murdered by Christian militiamen at a mosque and Islamic boarding school.[47] Many of those interviewed lost relatives at Walisongo. Shortly following the Walisongo massacre, teachers and trainers from JI came to Poso. Some joined to directly avenge the loss of relatives; others were attracted to the group out of a sense of vengeful solidarity. One former Tanah Runtuh member explains,

> I joined the *jihad qital* in 2000 [after Walisongo]. I would like to retaliate against that attack because in principle all Muslims are brothers. . . . None of my relatives were killed. But at the time, we saw dead bodies thrown in the water in Poso. Everyone was furious. When JI came to Pak Haji Adnan's compound, he said this was togetherness. I wanted to join. I attended *taklim* [religious study] to deepen my religious understanding. Then I was given the oath.[48]

Among the interviewees from Jemaah Islamiyah, many of whom had first joined Darul Islam and were founding JI members, the leading pathway to entry (cited by fifteen respondents) was attendance at Islamic study circles and mass prayer led by specific radical notables. In some cases, friends in the study groups or classmates invited them to participate. One founding member of Jemaah Islamiyah and veteran of the Soviet-Afghan War explains,

> I was the leader of a drug gang. Then the Petrus killing started, and I fled to Banten, West Java. While in Banten, I met someone called Asep Sutardi. He was an incredible person. He guided me out of the darkness. Asep Sutardi was the nephew of a JI

commander, and his grandfather was Ajengan Masduki. It turned out I was mixing with people high up in the organization. Asep Sutardi held a *pengajian* [a religious study meeting]. It was by invitation only. Secret. I performed *istiqomah* [discovering the right path]. I regretted my past life, my dark path. I left it behind. I learned *tauhid* [the divine oneness of god] and *aqidah* [faith]. I also attended paramilitary training in West Java, where we learned martial arts, self-defense, and played sports. You had to go through the different levels, and I was doing it all step by step. This process went on for more than a year. I was then inducted by Pak Broto into Darul Islam. In 1981, I was offered the opportunity to go to Afghanistan.[49]

Others actively searched for knowledge about jihad or Islam and sampled various study circles until they found their way into a JI or Darul Islam affiliated circle. A former member of the Subur cell, a study circle affiliated with Noordin M. Top and Dr. Azhari Husin, the masterminds behind the second Bali bombing, explains this searching process.

I was interested in learning about jihad, ever since I saw TV news about jihads in Afghanistan, Mindanao, and Palestine. I attended many *pengajian*, but when I asked questions to the various *ustads* [teachers], their answers were unsatisfactory. They were just like the books printed for the general public. . . . I was searching for something outside those books. Then a friend from one *pengajian*, a high school friend, offered to bring me to a *pengajian* run by Pak Subur. He said it would satisfy my curiosity about jihad in a more practical way.[50]

It is important to note that Islamic study circles take place throughout Indonesia and the Islamic world. Attendance at study circles is not necessarily a radicalizing factor. What matters instead is the type of study circle. Some are notorious because leaders espouse a particularly militant jihadist-Salafi viewpoint. It is these study circles that I am referring to in this book.

Another important pathway to entry, particularly among Java-based interviewees, was kinship ties or what Sidney Jones terms "inherited jihadism."[51] In Indonesia, going back to the era prior to independence, radical Islamist groups have always been present on the fringe, beginning with Darul Islam. JI was a breakaway faction of Darul Islam. It is thus possible for a family to have a grandfather who participated in Darul Islam in the independence era, a father who fought in Afghanistan as part of the Darul Islam contingent, a son in JI, and grandchildren in JI schools. Blood ties, marital ties, and extended kinship ties have all been factors in the radicalization of Indonesian militants. Among those interviewed, four came from such multigenerational jihadi families, and another two followed elder siblings into JI or one of its affiliates. It is important to note that the process of radicalization in these families is not simply a passive process of intergenerational indoctrination. Instead, the path can often be more deliberate, with JI members attempting to ensure their children are raised with the proper worldview via enrolling them in JI-affiliated preschool playgroups, Quran study groups, Islamic elementary schools, and Islamic boarding schools (*pesantren*).[52] This education model also serves to construct an extended family whose members, although not bonded by blood, are connected via their common ideology and experiences.

One such example is the late Abdul Rauf, who joined ISIS and died in Ramadi, Iraq, in April 2014. Abdul Rauf attended the infamous Al Mukmim (Ngruki) *pesantren*, established by JI's founders, Abdullah Sungkar and Abu Bakar Ba'asyir. His uncle Kang Jaja had established Ring Banten, a violent breakaway faction of Darul Islam. He explained the interaction effect between family and education in pushing him to join. "I joined because my family was there. There were soft pressures too, especially through what was said to me. [Things like] 'you studied at Ngruki, right?'"[53] It was expected he would join. It is important to note that attendance at Ngruki and other like-minded boarding schools should not be taken as proxy for membership into JI or its affiliates. However, at various points, recruiters used the schools as fertile ground to attract new members.

There is also significant variation in the levels and type of education received by interviewees. While twenty-two finished high school, sixteen furthered their studies in either vocational school, college, or graduate school. In Poso, the outbreak of communal conflict in 1999 caused seven respondents to terminate their studies at middle school or, in one instance, elementary school. While one might assume that participants in jihadist groups would be more likely to attend radical Islamist boarding schools, or conversely, to have little formal Islamic education—thus being more susceptible to indoctrination—those interviewed reflect a variety of experiences with Islamic education. While nineteen attended Islamic schools for at least some portion of their education, twenty-six went to public schools exclusively. Of those who attended Islamic schools, a minority, only six, attended radical Islamist boarding schools. The remainder attended state-run madrasas (Islamic day schools) or those run by local mass religious organizations like Muhammadiyah or al Chairat.

There is also significant variation in terms of participation in acts of violence. All but one participated in *jihad qital* (war) either in Afghanistan during the Soviet-Afghan War or the Southern Philippines during the Moro conflicts, in Syria, or locally in Ambon or Poso during the communal conflicts in those regions of Indonesia between 1999 and 2002.[54] Many participated in more than one *jihad qital*. If we understand a terrorist attack as an act of indiscriminate violence targeting civilians, including women and children, of course one can participate in terrorist acts in the context of a *jihad qital*. But it does not therefore follow that all participants in *jihad qital* inevitably commit terror actions. For some, especially among the Afghan veterans, combat experience more closely resembled that of soldiers in war. In fact, of those who participated in *jihad qital* in Afghanistan, in particular, a majority of those interviewed were flatly opposed to terror attacks and drew a stark line between bombings of malls, churches, bars, and hotels and the training and combat activities they participated in during the Soviet-Afghan War. Yet we would be remiss not to note that the chief architects of and many key participants in the Christmas Eve bombings, the Philippine ambassador bombing, the Atrium bombing, and the Bali bombing were also Afghan veterans.

Of those interviewed, twenty-four were directly involved in a specific terrorist attack (bombings, assassinations, mutilations, etc.), while another twenty-six played supporting roles in the organization (web development, logistics, transportation, robbery and other forms of "fund-raising," publishing, etc.) but did not play a direct role in terror actions. Many of those who played indirect roles in terror actions were not aware of the specifics of the attacks in which they were taking part. Someone who was told to pick up a car and drive it to a location was not necessarily told that the car was to be used in a bombing. It is also important to note that one's role often varied from operation to operation. Someone might have helped build a bomb for one operation or supply explosive materials but be tasked to rent a car for another without necessarily being told why. Roles were often not constant across operations.

All those interviewed for the study were male, for JI did not use women in its operations, nor did women participate in jihad experiences. Women in JI circles were expected to take care of the children and supplement the family economy. Over the course of this research, I conversed with four jihadi wives: two with husbands in JI and two with husbands in Tanah Runtuh. However, these talks were not conducted as formal interviews.[55] Interestingly, there is evidence that this gender exclusiveness is changing. ISIS affiliates in Southeast Asia are using women in a far more direct way than JI had. Women are becoming recruiters, propagandists, and even suicide bombers. However, this was not occurring at the time the research was being conducted for this book.

Finally, the interviewees are almost evenly divided between those who disengaged via shifting to a nonviolent role within the movement and those who disengaged via departure or going inactive. Another four remained hard-line and showed no evidence of embarking on a trajectory of disengagement. They were ready to commit violence again against their perceived enemy, should the opportunity present itself.

1

The Rise, Decline, and Resurgence of Jemaah Islamiyah

The purpose of this chapter is to chart the rise, retrenchment, and resurgence of Jemaah Islamiyah. In doing so, however, it will be necessary to address JI as part of a long-standing Indonesian fringe that imagined Indonesia as an Islamic state and was willing to use violence to make that a reality. At its height prior to the first Bali bombing in 2002, it had a membership of close to two thousand;[1] by 2010, those numbers were estimated to have fallen to two hundred.[2] By 2014, according to Indonesian police estimates derived from interrogations, its membership had climbed back to the pre-Bali bombing levels.[3] It is important to note at the outset of this chapter that Jemaah Islamiyah was never united by a common view of the conditions under which violence is permissible. Instead, it is more apropos to view JI as a network that splintered off from a preexisting terrorist group, only to have more radical factions splinter off from it. Moreover, it was and is also part of a larger community of jihadist groups within Indonesia. This chapter will touch on this broader community as well.

In order to address Jemaah Islamiyah's origins, we must first take a few pages to contextualize JI as a spinoff of Darul Islam. JI's founders came from Darul Islam. Those who went to fight in Afghanistan during the Soviet-Afghan War did so as part of Darul

Islam. Thus, we must take the time to understand those aspects of Darul Islam that laid the foundation for the emergence of JI.

Darul Islam is the name given to a series of rebellions in the provinces of Aceh, West Java, and South Sulawesi that sought to establish an Islamic state in Indonesia in the decades immediately following independence. Darul Islam disagreed with what it perceived as the secular basis of the nation that arose with the promulgation of the national ideology known as Pancasila.[4] At its height in the late 1950s, Darul Islam controlled or partially controlled swaths of villages in West Java and governed them according to its understanding of Islamic law. However, the revolt ultimately failed because Darul Islam lacked the necessary financial resources, which led its members to resort to armed robberies, looting, and various taxes levied on the villages it controlled, in order to fund its operations.[5] These activities alienated the public in those villages, which offered the government a means of entry by providing food and medical care in areas impacted by war.[6] The public backlash and government tactics would eventually lead to the rebel group's temporary implosion. When Darul Islam leader Sekarmadji Maridjan Kartosuwirjo was captured in 1962, and thirty-two of his top lieutenants renounced their struggle and pledged loyalty to the state in return for amnesty, Darul Islam went quiet.[7]

Less than a decade later, in 1971, Indonesian intelligence (BAKIN) funded a Darul Islam reunion, after several Darul Islam leaders professed privately that they would throw their support behind the dictator Suharto's personal political party, Golkar.[8] While Darul Islam had ceased to function as a movement during this decade, it continued to exist as a community bound by friendships, marriages, and familial ties. Propelled by the idea of this community voting in a bloc for Golkar and thus siphoning off votes from its Islamist rival, the United Development Party (PPP),

BAKIN permitted the reunion to go forward. It was no surprise that on the sidelines of the official speeches, these supporters held discussions about reviving the old networks, and at the subsequent Mahoni meeting, they chose new leaders.[9] The leadership took a long-term vision of their struggle, believing that while Darul Islam should wage jihad to bring about an Islamic state, it was necessary to first recruit more members and then accumulate sufficient resources and training to bring it about.

The Recruitment Drive

By 1975, Darul Islam had begun a recruitment drive, targeting youths and Muslim activists outside the movement.[10] As part of this effort, Darul Islam's leaders reformulated the movement's doctrines to emphasize *tauhid* (the divine oneness of God) and its political implications for governance. In doing so, they drew on Islamic texts from outside Indonesia, notably the work of the Egyptian Muslim Brotherhood, Pakistan's Maulana Mawdudi, and Syed Qutb. This emphasis on *tauhid* enabled Darul Islam to appeal to modernist Muslims,[11] for whom the concept is particularly resonant and who were struggling to maintain a political voice in Suharto's "New Order" regime. From 1967 onward, the Suharto regime took a series of steps that alienated Muslim modernists in particular. First, the regime refused to relegalize Masyumi,[12] the modernist Islamist party of the independence era that advocated most vociferously for both an Islamic state and adherence to democratic practices. Second, in 1973, the regime forced the amalgamation of the four Islamic parties, Parmusi, Nahdlatul Ulama, the Islamic Educational Movement (Perti), and the Indonesian Islamic Union Party (PSII), into one political party, thus eliminating the ability of the modernists to claim political space for their own agenda. That same year, Muslim–government relations would worsen after the People's Consultative Assembly, the upper legislative house, proposed two controversial regulations. The first would have put traditional Javanese beliefs on par with Islam and other established religions. The second would have standard-ized regulations on marriage and divorce by curtailing polygamy and removing marriage and divorce from the purview of Islamic courts.[13] Islamists took both these regulations as a gross insult, but the position of the regime had been duly conveyed. Muslims seek-ing the implementation of Islamic law could no longer work for that goal within the political system; but Darul Islam's ideology and activities enabled them to work outside the system.

The majority of recruits from that period came from the mod-ernist organizations: from Muhammadiyah; the Indonesian Is-lamic Students (Pelajar Islam Indonesia, or PII); the Islamic Youth Movement (Gerakan Pemuda Indonesia, or GPI); and the Indo-nesian Islamic Dakwah Council (Dewan Dakwah Islamiyah Indo-nesia, or DDII).[14] Two notable recruits during this period would go on to become Jemaah Islamiyah's founders, Abu Bakar Ba'asyir and Abdullah Sungkar. It is notable that both Sungkar and Ba'asyir had been active in GPI, perhaps indicating that they might have joined a vital, active Masyumi, rather than a clandestine Darul Islam, had such an outlet been available.

With a large influx of new members, Darul Islam's leaders dis-cussed commencing a jihad against the government. In 1976 and 1977, the Medan branch, under the leadership of Gaos Taufik, formed a jihad organization, which carried out various acts of terror specifically targeting churches and entertainment venues. Another Darul Islam member, "Warman," and a group of his asso-ciates also embarked on a campaign of *fai*—robbing "unbelievers" to fund the group's activities.[15] In the aftermath of the bombings and robberies, the perhaps inevitable crackdown ensued. It had become clear to officials in BAKIN that they had lost control of Darul Islam.[16]

In the 1980s, the Suharto regime's approach to political Islam grew even more hostile. The 1985 Pancasila as Azas Tunggal law required all parties to take the national ideology of Pancasila as their sole foundation. This meant that the United Development Party (PPP), the Islamist competitor to Suharto's Golkar party, was forced to remove all references to Islam from its charter and its symbols. The ruling was then extended to NGOs, mass organizations, and social movements. Some groups split over the issue, most notably the Indonesian Students Association (HMI), while others either acquiesced to the law or went underground. Muslims criticized the increasing appropriation of Pancasila by the regime for its own purposes. One particular flashpoint was the Tanjung Priok massacre, where police opened fire on Muslims protesting the desecration of an antigovernment mosque by a police officer. It was in this environment that Darul Islam adopted the *usroh* structure.

Amid the crackdown, as early as 1981, Darul Islam attempted to adapt to the newly restrictive environment by adopting the cell structure pioneered by the Egyptian Muslim Brotherhood. They formed small *usroh*, of ten to fifteen members each, all of whom were dedicated to living according to Islamic law.[17] This new method of organizing was secretive and more suited to a repressive political environment that was hostile to political Islam. It was also particularly useful at a time when much of the Darul Islam leadership was in prison, for the *usroh* structure did not require strong central authority. According to the International Crisis Group,

> the *usroh* transformed Darul Islam and gave it new energy and a sense of purpose. To the young activists, expanding the *usroh*

movement was not just a religious activity. It was a means toward the end of overthrowing the [Suharto] government and establishing an Islamic state, and as the number of recruits increased, that goal seemed more reasonable.[18]

Abdullah Sungkar and Abu Bakar Ba'asyir employed the *usroh* organizing method and used it as a means of recruiting and training new members.[19] Sungkar and Ba'asyir also founded the al Mu'mim boarding school in the village of Ngruki, near Solo, and started a radio program criticizing the government. The two leaders were in and out of prison throughout the late 1970s and early 1980s for their activities. In 1985, the Indonesian Supreme Court prepared to rule against Sungkar and Ba'asyir in a long-standing subversion case; the two decided to flee. After traveling to Saudi Arabia and Pakistan, they settled in Malaysia with a handful of followers and maintained a system of couriers who would go back and forth to Indonesia.[20]

Becoming Mujahidin: Darul Islam Goes to the Afghan Front

With the escalation of the Soviet-Afghan War, Abdullah Sungkar and Abu Bakar Ba'asyir became the conduit for recruits who wanted to fight in the jihad against the Soviets. During their travels to Pakistan, the two men built a relationship with Abdul Rasul Sayaaf; he agreed to take on their recruits, sending them for training first at his camp, Harby Pohantum Mujahidin Afghanistan al Ittihad al Islamy, and later at As Sadaah. In total, Ba'asyir and Sungkar would send ten batches of recruits between 1985 and 1991. The Indonesian government contends that 360 Indonesians were sent to train in Pakistan and Afghanistan.[21] Recruits were drawn from several sources: their *usroh* networks, Ngruki alumni, individuals from Darul Islam families, Darul Islam members outside their *usroh*, and personal contacts.[22] Over their tours, the fighters were taught field engineering, logistics, communications, map reading, weapons, basic infantry tactics, and explosives and bomb making. They also came into contact with Islamist fighters from other regions. Imam Samudra, one of the masterminds of the first Bali bombing, explains the lure of the camps:

> I did target practice with Kalashnikovs, M16s, handgun shooting, anti-tank grenade practice, grenade throwing and making bombs. . . . In Afghanistan, I met and was exposed to Islamic movements from all sorts of countries. . . . I met with the Muslim Brotherhood, the Egyptian Islamic Group, the Egyptian Jihad Group and so on, they were all in Afghanistan.[23]

The shared experience of training and living in Afghanistan bonded the Darul Islam members who participated, even though few took part in actual fighting at the front. The experience also exposed them to jihadi-Salafi ideology, notably its points on jihad. According to Solahudin, author of *The Roots of Terrorism in Indonesia*,

> In the understanding of Kartosuwirjo, Darul Islam's founder, jihad did not always mean *qital* or war. *Jihad* had a wider meaning: namely, all genuine efforts to do good deeds that accorded with Islam's teaching. . . .
> In Afghanistan, Darul Islam cadres were taught that the correct understanding of *jihad* was war [*qital*]. They were also taught different categories of *jihad*. There was offensive *jihad*, which was *fard al-kifaya*—that is, a collective rather than an individual obligation, meaning that as long as the goals could be achieved with a particular number of fighters, it was not obligatory for each and every Muslim to join in. And there was

defensive *jihad*, which was *fard al-ain*—obligatory for all Muslims. Defensive *jihad* was necessary when unbelievers attacked or occupied Muslim lands.[24]

The Soviet withdrawal from Afghanistan in 1989 felt like vindication for the Darul Islam jihadists; in their view, they had defeated a superpower.

Participation in the Soviet-Afghan War would have several net benefits for the group that would become JI. First, the Afghan veterans who would go on to form the core of JI were highly trained fighters bonded by their shared experiences and shared jihadi-Salafi worldview. Second, the relationships they built in the camps enabled them to form ties to other radical Islamist groups in Indonesia who also had Afghan veterans as founding members, as well as other jihadi-Salafi groups in Southeast Asia. This would prove useful, for example, when seeking out a location to build a training camp; they called upon friends in the Moro Islamic Liberation Front (MILF). Third, some of them had also built relationships with Middle Eastern and South Asian jihadist leaders in the camps. Hambali, a founding JI member and one of the leaders of the pro-bombing wing, had befriended Khaled Sheikh Mohammad, for example, who provided funds for several bombing operations and enabled thirty members to train at al Qaeda's camp al Faruq. Many would draw on what they learned in Afghanistan to demarcate their positions as pro- or anti-bombing during the debates to come.

Jemaah Islamiyah Splits from Darul Islam

In 1993, Abdullah Sungkar and his followers formally split from Darul Islam. Several reasons have been cited for the split, but they revolve around irreconcilable tensions between Darul

Islam's Imam Ajengan Masduki and Abdullah Sungkar. The most commonly cited reason is Sungkar's puritanical Salafism could not coexist with Masduki's Sufi tendencies.[25] Those Indonesians fighting in Afghanistan as the split was developing were given a choice: they could side with Sungkar or Masduki. Those who chose Masduki would be sent home, but those who chose Sungkar could stay in Afghanistan. Almost unanimously, the Indonesians sided with Sungkar.

Jemaah Islamiyah's emergence from Darul Islam had several interesting implications for the former's development. Importantly, JI's roots in Darul Islam have given rise to multigenerational jihadi families. That so many jihadists can cite their family history and familial legacy as having roots in the broader jihadi community creates a powerful sense of belonging.[26] Moreover, it also provides a level of unmatched loyalty, protection, and support that can make participation in high-risk and often illegal activities seem comparatively safe from infiltration; one can always find relatives who are willing to assist or offer refuge.[27] Sidney Jones highlights the potential of kinship ties in fostering the next generation of jihadists, noting that hundreds of terrorist detainees have siblings or children already in the movement.[28] The phenomenon of jihadi families creates extended kin networks bound by shared experience, ideological indoctrination beginning in preschool, marital ties, and family history. That makes disengagement via departure more difficult, for it implies breaking with familial tradition and perhaps alienating parents and elder siblings.

Additionally, Jemaah Islamiyah adopted certain concepts and tactics from Darul Islam, notably the concept of the secure base area (*qoidul aminah*) where Islamic law could be fully applied, and the tactic of using *fai*—robbery of unbelievers to fund jihad activities. JI attempted to put the concept of a secure base into practice in Poso between 2002 and 2007, following the end of the communal conflict in the region. Several JI members operating independently of the group and in conjunction with members of other violent Islamist extremist groups, notably Mujahidin KOMPAK, Ring Banten, and Abu Bakar Ba'asyir's new radical group, Jemaah Anshorut Tauhid (JAT), attempted to establish a secure base again in 2010 in Aceh, believing that the one province of Indonesia governed under Islamic law would be receptive to their goals. Both those attempts, which shall be discussed at some length below, ultimately failed.

Jemaah Islamiyah Builds a Structure

In Jemaah Islamiyah's initial years, the leadership was focused on creating an organizational structure that made sense and putting together a plan for how to achieve their goal of establishing an Islamic state in Indonesia. When Jemaah Islamiyah was initially formed in 1993, it had a lean administrative structure with two divisions: the first comprised Indonesia, and the second, Malaysia and Singapore.[29] When JI set up a military training camp, Camp Hudaibiyah, in Mindanao in the Southern Philippines in 1997, it added a third region. When the General Guidelines for Struggle (PUPJI) were drafted around the same time, their architects gave each of these three "Mantiqis" a core responsibility. Mantiqi 1 encompassed Malaysia and Singapore and was charged with fund-raising. Mantiqi 2 comprised large portions of Indonesia, apart from Papua, East Kalimantan, and Sulawesi, and was denoted as the recruitment region. Mantiqi 3 was the training region, composed of Sabah in East Malaysia, the Southern Philippines, and East Kalimantan and Sulawesi in

Indonesia.[30] However, when Mantiqi 1 collapsed with the arrests that followed the Bali bombing in 2002, and when the Philippine military overran MILF Camp Abu Bakar, ending access to Camp Hudaibiyah, Jemaah Islamiyah adapted to the more constricted environment. It abandoned the Mantiqi structure and reorganized its administrative and paramilitary structures into one centered on Indonesia. By 2005, decimated by arrests, JI adapted yet again, scaling back its military wing to a single unit led by Abu Dujana, with squads in Solo, Semarang, Jakarta, and Surabaya.

The PUPJI outlined the process by which JI would achieve an Islamic state in Indonesia.[31] It would be a multistage process. While the eventual jihad and the necessity of paramilitary training are highlighted in the document, so too is the cultivation of the Islamic individual, family, and group.[32] Before JI could mount its jihad to establish an Islamic state, it first had to cultivate a core leadership "who possess true faith, knowledge, leadership skills and adaptation mechanisms."[33] Then it would be necessary to build a solid base of followers, who would be obedient and dedicated to the group's cause. Islamic propagation (*dakwah*) and Islamic education (*tarbiyah*) were key components of this effort. It was also important to take steps to ensure Jemaah Islamiyah would remain a *tanzim siri*, or secret organization, given that it did intend to overthrow the government eventually and that its members were undertaking paramilitary training. Finally, JI needed to establish a secure base (*qoidul aminah*) that it could govern according to Islamic law and from which it could embark on armed struggle.[34] Members participated in the movement via teaching and learning, preaching, and joining in paramilitary training opportunities. However, engaging in acts of terrorism was not yet on the radar.

During this period and until the Bali bombing, Jemaah Islamiyah was able to conduct its activities quite openly in Southeast Asia. According to Greg Fealy, the period from 1999 to 2002 constituted an organizational "high point" in terms of membership and operations.[35] "They were able to recruit and train extensively."[36] JI held mass prayers and ran small religious study courses for the public as part of its *dakwah*. From there, the group selected certain individuals to attend exclusive religious study sessions, and if they came to understand all the materials and fulfilled all the membership criteria, they would be invited to join the movement, a process that took over a year.[37] After being invited into the organization, JI members would participate in paramilitary education, where students were taught survival skills, war tactics, map reading, and self-defense, as well as swimming and mountain climbing.[38] The best recruits during this period were sent to JI's Camp Hudaibiyah on Mindanao in the Southern Philippines, while others were sent to one of a dozen other camps throughout Indonesia. In the late 1990s, JI also sent thirty cadres to participate in paramilitary training at al Qaeda's al Faruq camp.[39] In the aftermath of September 11, 2001, security services in Malaysia and Singapore identified and arrested members of Mantiqi 1, but the network was still able to operate quite freely in Indonesia and the Philippines until the Bali bombing operation in October 2002.

The arrests that followed the Bali bombing, however, devastated both structural JI and its extra-institutional equivalents, resulting in the imprisoning of much of JI's leadership and membership between 2004 and 2010. Where does JI's near implosion begin? While one may be tempted to cite the Bali bombing, as this was the moment when JI was revealed as a network and arrests of key bombers were made, the shift began earlier, with the debates surrounding Osama bin Laden's 1998 fatwa.

The Debate over Osama bin Laden's Fatwa

The arrival of Osama bin Laden's "Jihad against the Jews and the Crusaders" in 1998 was a particular turning point in the ideational development of Jemaah Islamiyah. The fatwa invited Muslim fighters to shift their attention from attacking the near enemy (their home governments) to the far enemy (Western targets) and legitimated attacks on civilians. The document sparked a disagreement among JI's leaders about the suitability of the fatwa to the Indonesian context.[40] On the one hand, two senior members of Mantiqi 1, Hambali and Muchlas (founding members of JI who would go on to lead the pro-bombing faction and mastermind several attacks), were favorably inclined to the fatwa, contending that jihad against the United States and its allies should be a top priority, since the Americans were occupying Muslim lands. On the other hand, Mantiqi 2 seniors, led by Abu Rusdan and Achmad Roihan, rejected this view, asserting that fighting the "near enemy" (that is, the Indonesian government) took precedence over the "far enemy."[41] In the latter view, it was not advisable to take on the international system via a global jihad.[42] To bolster their case, the Mantiqi 2 seniors sought an opinion from Salamat Hashim, the head of the Moro Islamic Liberation Front, who stated, "The contents of the fatwa are good, but it is impossible to carry out in Mindanao because the conditions don't allow for it."[43] The Mantiqi 2 seniors felt the same argument applied to Indonesia.

Sidney Jones, director of the Institute for Policy Analysis of Conflict, suggests that the difference in position between the Malaysian and Indonesian members may be attributed to different political environments, with Malaysia under Mahathir being "more outward looking, rhetorically anti-Western and open to virtually every Muslim guerrilla group and liberation movement in the world."[44] In contrast, Indonesia lacked this openness, and as a result its members tended to focus their attentions on the ongoing domestic political struggle for an Islamic state.[45] The end of the Suharto dictatorship in 1998 and the outbreak of communal conflict in Maluku and Poso offered Indonesia-based JI members, many of whom were well-trained Afghan veterans, new opportunities for struggle that their brothers in Malaysia lacked. It was natural for them to focus on their home country.

The death of Sungkar in 1999 would have serious implications for this cleavage, as subsequent amirs lacked Sungkar's firmness. With JI's then-amir, Abu Bakar Ba'asyir, refusing to take steps to rein in the network's most radical elements, Mantiqi 1, with Hambali at the helm, circumvented the established leadership and carried out terrorist attacks, notably the bombing of a Medan church in 2000, the Christmas Eve bombings in 2000, an attempted bombing of a church inside the Atrium Mall in 2001, and the Bali bombing in 2002.

According to Nasir Abas, the former head of JI's training region, Mantiqi 3, the goal of the church attacks was to ignite a civil war between Christians and Muslims in Indonesia.[46] Solahudin concurs, noting Jemaah Islamiyah members believed that Christians would seek revenge for the church bombings, while alleging they stockpiled weapons in their churches.[47] Should the conflict escalate in this fashion, it would undoubtedly, they thought, benefit JI, as a host of Muslims would flock to the group.[48] However, the attacks did not ignite the desired Christian response; the Christians did not arm themselves. In fact, the Christmas Eve bombings led to an unintended consequence, as Muslim groups, including Nahdlatul Ulama, Muhammadiyah, and even radical Islamist vigilante militias like the Islamic Defenders Front (FPI) took it upon themselves in future years to guard churches to ensure such an attack would never happen again and their Christian brethren could pray in peace. Moreover, the action evoked the ire of JI's anti-bombing wing, which contended that it was premature to engage in jihad against the state. To do so before they had built a solid base of followers among the public and had established a secure base could have adverse consequences for JI.[49] In taking these steps, Hambali's group created a precedent for the most radical to go off and conduct their own actions. It was a move that would eventually split JI in two.[50]

It is important to note that the debate within JI circles was not over whether to use violence in pursuit of their goals. The anti-bombing wing within JI was not arguing that the movement should rely on nonviolent methods like *dakwah* (Islamic propagation) and *tarbiyah* (Islamic education) to the exclusion of violence. Instead, it is important to understand that the core dispute was one of disagreement over location, tactics, timing, and condition. In other words, should JI engage in jihad in the present era, or should it prioritize training its leaders and members and cultivating a support base for a jihad to come? When communal violence between Christians and Muslims broke out in Poso in December 1998 and Ambon in January 1999, however, both sides agreed that it was incumbent on JI to intervene to protect Muslims from Christian paramilitaries. The debate over when to embark on an antistate jihad was put aside; a legitimate local jihad had come to them.

Jemaah Islamiyah Joins the Communal Conflicts

After what began as episodic communal violence and rants, both the Maluku and Poso conflicts escalated. Both conflicts had their roots in economic insecurity and political anxieties in the aftermath of the fall of Suharto's thirty-two-year New Order dictatorship. Anxiety over control of and access to state patronage, combined with inadequate law enforcement, created the environment for violence.[51] Although neither conflict was ignited for religious reasons, both soon took on a religious hue, as mosques and churches were common targets. The greatest atrocities victimizing the Muslim side had overt religious links, notably "bloody Idul Fitri"[52] in Ambon in January 1999 and the May 2000 massacre of at least one hundred men and sexual assault of women at a mosque and Islamic boarding school at Walisongo.[53] These attacks and connections to faith, one on a major holiday and another at an Islamic boarding school, enabled outside forces to politicize a local conflict on religious grounds and call for a jihad to protect Muslims. Weak law enforcement exacerbated the violence,[54] facilitating the creation of a vacuum into which various jihadi groups could enter.

In June 1999, several months after bloody Idul Fitri, JI held a meeting to discuss the possibility of joining the Maluku conflict but did not put a concrete plan in motion. JI members interested in fighting in Maluku instead went there via Komite Aksi Penanggulangan Akibat Krisis (KOMPAK), a humanitarian aid organization under the auspices of Dewan Dakwah Islamiyah Indonesia (DDII). KOMPAK was the first to travel to Maluku. In October of 1999 it set up a humanitarian aid office and a paramilitary training session at Waimorat. Many JI members went to Maluku as part of KOMPAK initially, believing that JI was too slow in reacting to the conflict. Tensions would eventually mount between JI and KOMPAK because of overlapping roles. Initially, KOMPAK was tasked with humanitarian relief, while JI would fight. On the ground, however, both groups engaged in battle. Eventually, they would split. However, JI members would continue to fight as part of "Mujahidin KOMPAK" in both Maluku and Poso.

In Poso, in the weeks following the 2000 Walisongo massacre, trainers and fighters from Mujahidin KOMPAK and then JI began arriving. Mujahidin KOMPAK set up its base in the Kayamanya neighborhood, while JI trainers made inroads into Gebangrejo and Tanah Runtuh, forming an alliance with Haji Adnan Arsal, a senior religious figure based in the latter area. The primary difference between the two groups lay in their timeline for participation in jihad. Mujahidin KOMPAK offered a three-week course, focusing on paramilitary training. By contrast, JI required individuals commit to a month of religious indoctrination before some were selected to go on for further paramilitary training as well as continued religious study. KOMPAK's local followers adopted the name Mujahidin Kayamanya, after the neighborhood in which they were based. The JI-affiliated local group likewise referred to themselves as Tanah Runtuh, after their base neighborhood. The arrival of the jihadi militias marked a decisive shift in the conflict, providing the Muslim side with a significant military advantage during the fighting in 2001.[55]

In the course of the relationship between the local fighters and outside jihadis, each used the other for their own purposes. The local Poso fighters joined the "ustads from Java," as they knew the JI and KOMPAK teachers, seeking opportunities for revenge and finding refuge in an ideological frame of reference that would legitimate that desire. Jemaah Islamiyah saw Poso as a potential investment opportunity. Poso was a hilly and mountainous area with a fast-flowing river and easy access to the coast; thus, it was defensible. The portion of the Muslim population that had remained in Poso following the violence strongly supported JI's presence, and JI leaders reinforced this initial inclination by marrying into the community.[56] JI leaders realized that they could use Poso as a secure base, where they could implement Islamic law, socialize their message via *dakwah*, and generate income via the cacao trade.[57] The concept of the secure base featured prominently in JI discourses and in the PUPJI; it was a legacy of JI's history as part of Darul Islam. In the aftermath of the 2001 Malino peace accords, as the fighting between Muslim and Christian militias died down and as Hambali's faction focused on bombings, the anti-bombing wing focused on the cultivation of that base.

Between 2001 and January 2007, JI maintained a secure base in Poso, for much of that time without attracting the attention of local authorities. Project Uhud, as it was called, was first under the auspices of Abu Tholut, then the head of Mantiqi 3; it was then passed on to his successor, Nasir Abas, who sought to use the territory to cultivate an economic base for JI.[58] Abas then tasked Hasanuddin, a JI member who had formerly fought with the Moro Islamic Liberation Front in Mindanao, with the day-to-day operations in the area.[59] By 2005, Poso was critical for JI's continued efforts to finance its activities and pay for the upkeep of spouses and children of its members who were in prison.[60] Money from armed robberies provided an important supplemental source of income.

After Abas's arrest in 2003, Hasanuddin began to depart from Abas's agenda, fueled by the desire for revenge among the Poso jihadis under his command. This subgrouping within Tanah Runtuh, denoted as the hit squad, carried out a series of attacks between 2003 and 2006, mostly targeting Christians. The hit squad attacks included the killing of thirteen Christian villagers in Poso and Morowali by masked gunmen in October 2003; the bombing of a minivan in November 2004 that killed six people; the May 2005 Tentena market bombing that killed twenty-three; the mutilation of three schoolgirls in October 2005; the bombing of the Palu market on December 31, 2005, which left eight dead; and two homemade bombs that killed a man and a woman in 2006.[61]

Approximately 150 people, the majority of whom were Christians, were killed between 2003 and 2006 in the revenge attacks.[62]

In January 2007, after several months of negotiations between the police, intermediaries, and the jihadis, Densus 88, the police antiterrorism team, raided JI's base at Tanah Runtuh. The impact of the raid was shattering for both JI and Tanah Runtuh. During the raid itself, sixteen people were killed, over a dozen more arrested, and the police seized a large cache of factory-made weapons and explosives.[63] Those Tanah Runtuh fighters who were not arrested or killed went on the run. In the aftermath, some sixty-four JI members were picked up by the police, including the interim amir, Zarkasih.[64] JI lost its secure base. The majority of its leaders were now in prison. In the aftermath of the raids, JI entered a period of consolidation, shifting away from militancy, toward education and Islamic propagation for the time being.

The Bombing Campaign and JI's Decline

At the same time Jemaah Islamiyah fighters were participating in jihad in Maluku and Poso, Hambali's faction embarked on a bombing campaign, first targeting churches in an attempt to ignite a civil war between Muslims and Christians and then attacking symbols of Western influence. The bombing campaign had lasting impacts on JI's cohesion as both a community and an organizational network. Most notably, it divided JI into pro-bombing and anti-bombing factions, the former supporting the use of terror attacks in pursuit of an Islamic state and Islamic law, and the latter holding that violence should be restricted to conflict zones like Afghanistan, Ambon, Poso, and Mindanao in which Muslims were under threat.

Regardless of whether their members were pro- or anti-bombing, however, both groups supported participation in the jihads in Maluku and Poso. Ali Imron, Umar Patek, Amrozi, Dulmatin, and other Bali bombing participants also fought in Ambon. One should not assume the two groups were separate or that they did not interact with each other. Instead, it would be more appropriate to see the pro-bombing faction as participating in JI's leadership, its organizational structure, its religious activities, and its jihad activities. In their zeal to mount bombings in pursuit of their goals, however, they also undermined the structure in which they participated by sidestepping it to carry out their attacks.

The key incident that escalated Jemaah Islamiyah's trajectory of decline was the first Bali bombing. On October 12, 2002, one suicide bomber exploded a backpack bomb in Paddy's Bar while another detonated a car bomb in front of the Sari Club. In total, 202 people were killed and 300 were injured in the attacks. The investigation that followed the Bali bombing revealed JI as a network. Moreover, the clampdown that followed netted the key figures in Mantiqi 1 who had planned and perpetrated the attack (Muchlas, Amrozi, Imam Samudra, Ali Imron); individuals with indirect or tangential involvement; and then other JI figures who had any knowledge of the attack, sat in on meetings, or helped a member flee.[65] The crackdown then extended to other JI figures who had not been involved, including Achmad Roihan, Abu Rusdan, Abu Tholut, and Nasir Abas. Umar Patek and Dulmatin went on the run, seeking refuge in the Southern Philippines. Long prison sentences were meted out to those who played minor roles, while life sentences and death sentences were handed down to those who either planned or helped carry out the attack.

Such consequences generated considerable resentment among the JI rank and file. Many JI members saw the costs outweighing the benefits and criticized Muchlas and Imam Samudra for masterminding the operation.[66] While these factions of JI remained formally in the same movement, the split between them had become irreconcilable. With the arrest of Hambali in Thailand in 2003, this faction was taken over by Malaysian nationals, Noordin M. Top and Dr. Azhari Husin. Following in the footsteps of Hambali, Imam Samudra, and Muchlas, Noordin Top plotted a series of bombing operations against symbols of Western influence. These include the Australian Embassy bombing in 2004, the second Bali bombing in 2005, and the Marriott and Ritz-Carlton Hotel bombings in 2009.

Noordin Top justified his actions based on the argument that in a time of emergency, a small group, or even individuals, could take matters into their own hands and take on an enemy without consulting and winning the support of their imam.[67] This ran counter to the argument within mainstream JI circles that large-scale bombings were counterproductive for the organization's long-term survival and its ability to win support among the broader populace for its goals. Even before the Australian Embassy bombing in 2004, the leaders of JI's anti-bombing wing had decided it was permissible for JI members to inform on Noordin Top and his counterpart, the master bomb maker, Azhari Husin, if they had information about where either man was staying.[68] The split between JI and the Noordin–Azhari faction was formalized when Noordin began calling his group "al Qaeda in the Malay Archipelago" and "al Qaeda in Southeast Asia," titles pointing to his admiration of al Qaeda rather than any direct affiliation.

It is important to note that Noordin Top's group never constituted a formal organization. Instead, it is better to conceive of it as a cell with an ever-changing membership. Each time Noordin sought to mount an operation, he sought out individuals interested in participating, first among hard-liners in JI and, over time, increasingly from other jihadist groups, notably Mujahidin KOMPAK and Ring Banten.[69] Thus, whenever too many members were either arrested or killed, he just recruited new ones. Each operation typically required a new set of recruits. The pace of Noordin's operations would slow considerably following the killing of his partner, Azhari Husin, in 2005. Noordin Top himself was killed by authorities in a seventeen-hour siege in 2009. Since then, there have been no major bombing attacks against Western targets, although church bombings and actions targeting police or police posts by small, often unaffiliated cells remain common.

The actions of the pro-bombing splinter groups were having serious adverse effects on JI. Fifteen years ago, JI was a hierarchical network with cells in Indonesia, Malaysia, Singapore, the Philippines, and Australia. The arrests that followed the first Bali bombing and subsequent investigations leading to the arrest, imprisonment, or killing of key JI figures between 2004 and 2010 decimated "structural" JI as well as the pro-bombing factions.[70] In the aftermath, JI's members were mostly confined to Indonesia. Its activities consisted mainly of study groups in key cities, including Solo, Semarang, Lampung, Jakarta, and Palu, each led by a specific charismatic cleric, as well as forty affiliated schools.[71] The 2007 Densus 88 raids in Poso, the arrest of key JI leaders and members, and the end of Project Uhud forced a pause in the JI community. Its refusal to mount a reprisal operation, according to Sidney Jones, delegitimized it as a militant organization in the eyes of other radical groups.[72]

In the arrests that followed the January 2007 Densus raids in Poso, JI became a shadow of its former self, retaining little of its former reach, organization, or cohesion. Mujahidin KOMPAK was effectively a dead organization. Abu Bakar Ba'asyir, former amir of JI, started a new organization, Jemaah Anshorut Tauhid (JAT), which quickly supplanted JI as the most influential and cohesive Islamist extremist group, with entire branches of JI joining JAT. Tanah Runtuh splintered, as those who sought to continue violence first joined JAT and then a new jihadi group calling itself Mujahidin Indonesia Timor (MIT, or East Indonesia Holy Warriors), led by a former Tanah Runtuh member, Santoso.

For about half a decade following the 2007 Densus 88 raids, JI focused on *dakwah*, recruitment, and organizational development at the expense of paramilitary training, preparations for war (*i'dad*), or terror attacks. Going back prior to 2007, there was a ban on conducting terror attacks outside of Poso. One JI member recalled a superior telling him around 2007, "Brother, I am not going to think about *amaliyah* [actions] for the next fifteen years. We're more focused on putting the network in order. If we cannot stop you from *amaliyah*, we will send you abroad."[73] For some former members of Jemaah Islamiyah, there was little attraction in continuing participation in a militant group that did little in the way of paramilitary training, preparations for war, or terror actions.

The 2010 Lintas Tanzim project was the most ambitious action of the period. It was an attempt by disgruntled members of JI, Mujahidin KOMPAK, Ring Banten, and JAT to take matters into their own hands, seize momentum, and ultimately establish a secure base in Aceh, the one province of Indonesia under sharia. They sought an area under their control that would serve as a refuge, a base of operations, and a military training camp.[74] While JI's leadership had no hand in the operation, Dulmatin, a former member of JI and one of its most infamous bombers still at large, led the initiative. The camp was bankrolled by JAT. Viewing Noordin Top's strategy of large-scale bombings as inadvisable because of the inevitable backlash, they preferred targeted assassinations of civilian, police, and military officials, as well as anyone spreading "secular ideals" in the base area. They would fail, however, as their training camp was discovered by local police, and the Police Mobile Brigade (Brimbob) launched an operation to arrest the jihadists, who, after a brief attempt to hold their ground, fled.[75]

During this period overall, terror attacks continued, but they were far smaller in scale, mostly targeting the police or churches and carried out by cells affiliated with JAT, disgruntled JI members, or independent actors inspired by radical preachers. In 2010, Mujahidin Indonesia Timor (MIT) would take up the goal of the secure base, drawing disaffected followers from Tanah Runtuh, the Poso branch of JAT, and JI. They would hold a small sliver of mountain territory until mid-2016, when the police killed their head, Santoso. Further arrests of MIT members came in the ensuing months, including the second-in-command, Basri, alias Bagong.

Jemaah Islamiyah Resurgent

The decision to cease the use of violence as a strategy in Indonesia, at least for the time being, does not mean that JI's underlying goals and eventual plans for a revolution have changed. Instead, JI has been working to rebuild its network and capacities, recognizing that it lacks the ability to successfully take on the Indonesian state. As early as 2008 and 2009, Jemaah Islamiyah began quietly rebuilding itself first on Java and then on other islands. It held study circles and *pengajian* and began sending its preachers (*dai*) to even the most remote areas, including Papua, East Nusa Tenggara, and Flores.[76] By 2014, police were estimating JI's membership at two thousand again, the number it had prior to the first Bali bombing in 2002.[77] No one can be sure of the exact membership numbers, but JI is recruiting. According to a spokesman from the

JI affiliate Majlis Dakwah Ummat Islam (MDUI, or Islamic Propagation Council for the Islamic Community) in 2011 from Klaten, "There are 65 places outside Java where we're sending preachers."[78] They were actively recruiting among university students and targeting well-educated professionals, including chemical engineers, communications specialists, doctors, and nuclear technicians.[79] The 2014 Jemaah Islamiyah strategic plan stated that it had recruited a total of 132 university-educated professionals; it had set a target of 2,950.[80] JI has held monthly outdoor physical fitness and map-reading training sessions, including one where participants learned to assemble, disassemble, and fire an M-16 rifle. Financially, JI is in a better state, able to pay subsidies to the families of its members serving time in prison.[81] JI also has a new organizational structure, with five western sectors across Java and Sumatra and two eastern ones.[82]

JI has also taken an interest in the conflict in Syria. Going back to 2010, the Hilal Ahmar Society Indonesia (HASI), JI's humanitarian wing, has organized delegations to Syria, with senior JI members taking part.[83] Abu Rusdan, JI's spiritual leader, has stated that it was time for Indonesia to join the global jihad and that "thinking small" and focusing on the local jihad has only "sapped their strength" because there was always a stronger force ready to defeat them.[84] Consequently, JI has become increasingly committed to using the Syrian experience as an opportunity for those members who want to fight to gain the training and experience they cannot get at home. JI has tended to support the al Qaeda affiliate Jabhat Fateh el Shams, over ISIS, whereas JAT, MIT, and Aman Abdurrahman's followers have sided with ISIS. JI's initial forays into Syria took the form of provision of humanitarian relief assistance. Between 2012 and 2013, JI held some sixty discussions and fundraising events to raise money for humanitarian aid, funneling it through its relief arm, HASI.[85] It sent interested members on monthlong trips. At the conclusion of their tour, some members slipped away to join Jabhat Fateh el Shams or, less frequently, ISIS, viewing the opportunity to participate in a legitimate jihad as too good to pass up.

This provides an interesting environment for those who track disengaging jihadists. As JI has become more organized and active, and as there is now a venue for those seeking to fight in a legitimate jihad abroad, who will choose to go from inactive to active? Who will reengage, and under what conditions? Chapter 2 will examine the process by which individual jihadists from JI, Mujahidin KOMPAK, Tanah Runtuh, and Mujahidin Kayamanya are disengaging from violence and, importantly, the factors that are most likely to lead to successful reintegration.

2

Patterns of Disengagement

When jihadists discuss how they came to disengage from violence, they often assert it begins as a gradual process of introspection in which they reflect on what they have done and contemplate whether they have diverged from the "correct path," what in Islam is termed *muhasabah*. However, they often admit that something external brought it on: perhaps they participated in an action that did not quite feel right; statements by certain hard-line friends seemed irrational, impractical, or just far too intolerant; they were hit with the nagging sense that "things had just gone too far"[1] in terms of violence; they were dismayed when they found that their leaders misled them regarding a particular operation and their role in it; or they felt shame or guilt when seeing their parents cry for the first time upon hearing their son was among Indonesia's most wanted.

That initial spark by itself does not lead to disengagement. The opening may close. It may also lead to questioning, reflection, reading, and discussion. An individual may turn to the Quran to review the verses governing conduct during war. Someone who had received an education from Nahdlatul Ulama or Muhammadiyah or al Chairat schools may turn back to his prior education and look to those texts, lessons, and teachers. A former member of the Tarbiyah movement in the 1980s and 1990s might revisit the ideas, methods, values, and priorities espoused in its study circles.

In addition to turning inward, individuals may also seek clarification and understanding from outside sources, seeking out like-minded in-group friends to air their concerns, or discussing their misgivings with new people who can bring in alternative perspectives. There may be many such conversations. Those who sought out friends within the movement often found, to their surprise, that others shared their feelings. There is a prominent stream within JI and especially among a segment of the Afghan veterans that believes bombings against civilian targets are not only counterproductive to the movement's overall goals but also un-Islamic. Drawing on the standard understanding of *jihad qital*, they contend that jihad should be confined to conflict zones and that Indonesia is not the appropriate location for such actions. Moreover, now is not the time for the jihadis to go to war to build an Islamic state in Indonesia. It is far better to focus on educating the population regarding the suitability of an Islamic state than to bomb civilians willy-nilly, commit the sin of possibly killing Muslims, and alienate the population at large who find bombings reprehensible. If one is so inspired by the spirit of jihad, they contend, better to go fight in Syria, on a "legitimate field of battle." Haven't the costs of the bombings, exacted in arrests, loss of materials, resources, and freedom of movement, proven their unsuitability?

Over time, other factors may reinforce those initial reflections, thoughts, and feelings, one building on another, rational and emotional, through introspection and interaction, until the individual migrates from a violent to a nonviolent role within the movement; falls back to participate in minimal activities such as religious study or celebration; goes "inactive"; or breaks with the movement altogether. In Indonesia, however, even those who leave the group may still maintain friendships with fellow jihadists, especially if they are like-minded with regard to disapproval of bombings and acts of terrorism against civilians.

Disengagement Unpacked

In more than one hundred interviews conducted between 2010 and 2016 with fifty-five people, four factors were raised repeatedly as key to disengagement. First, many felt disillusioned and disappointed with certain aspects of the movement, most often the tactics and the leaders of the movement but occasionally their own actions, the ideology they were taught, hard-line friends, or the younger generations of militants. Second, rational assessment of context, conditions, and cost and benefits was frequently mentioned. These two factors were often part of an inward reflective process. Third, relationships with individuals outside the jihadi network, whether friends, family, or mentors, were key not only to disengagement but also to efforts at reintegration. This makes logical sense. If an individual is going to put distance between himself and his old social network, an alternative social circle of friends, family, and colleagues can help in conceptualizing and realizing a post-jihad life. Finally, changing personal and professional priorities also played a key role by reinforcing disengagement and, crucially, reintegration (see figure 2).

As interviewees reflected on their disengagement trajectory, they often mentioned that the process began for them with a sense of disillusionment or disappointment with the tactics and leaders of their respective movements. Specifically, they expressed opposition to the type of attack (bombings); the targets of the violence (civilians); the location of attacks (Indonesia); and the timing of attacks (the current era). There was a general sense that things

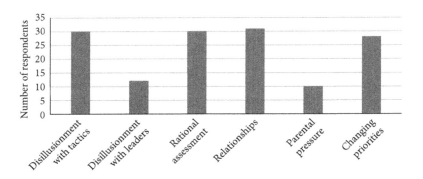

FIGURE 2
Factors leading to disengagement

had gone too far when Hambali and Mantiqi 1 masterminded the bombing campaigns. One ex-JI Afghan veteran simply stated, "There was too much violence. It was not right."[2]

A little more than a third also expressed disillusionment with specific leaders, whom they saw as "weak," "poor strategists," "unwilling to listen to reason," or "too dogmatic," and for marshaling rhetoric at odds with their own personal behavior.[3] Of the individuals interviewed, thirty condemned the bombing tactics and twelve condemned the leaders. The leader most frequently criticized was the former amir of JI, Abu Bakar Ba'asyir, who was referred to as "weak," "not self-aware," "not responsible," "not loyal," and "not firm."[4] In several narratives, this disillusionment was the starting point, where interviewees began to have nagging reservations regarding either the actions of the group or of what was being demanded of them. One Indonesian veteran of the Soviet-Afghan War and founding JI member expressed his disappointment with tactics:

> I did not agree with the bombings. They targeted civilians. In Islam, you are forbidden from doing that. It is not gentlemanly. In

Afghanistan, it was a gentleman's war. We fought soldiers. Same in the Philippines. Kashmir. We were not fighting civilians.

You know [Imam] Samudra? He was one of my men. He said, "Let's return to Indonesia and do jihad there with wealth and our souls." Do they have money? No money. Then, I heard he had been robbing people in Banten. I felt apprehensive. I felt sorry for him, but what could I do? He had chosen his path. A year later, he launched the bombing campaign in Jakarta, the church bombing ... and until the Bali bombing. . . . I had already returned to Indonesia from Malaysia by that time. Since then, I became disappointed.[5]

This particular veteran had been close to JI's founders, Abdullah Sungkar and Abu Bakar Ba'asyir. He had fought in Afghanistan. Disillusionment played profoundly into his decision to disengage. He draws a distinct line between the "gentleman's jihad" in a proper theater of battle like Afghanistan and the use of terror tactics against civilian targets. This disapproval of the latter alienated him from Hambali's faction. He was disappointed that Hambali and Mantiqi 1 took JI in such a destructive direction.

I was not disappointed in the JI leadership but in Mantiqi 1, which was in Hambali's hand. It was not intended to be [this way], but our headquarters were also in his hand. This was the beginning of the radicalism. . . . Many of our colleagues disagreed with the course taken. Just imagine, we learned military skills for fourteen years, only to be deceived. . . . The goal was to turn Indonesia into an Islamic state, but this was hijacked by Hambali.[6]

Emotions like disillusionment and disappointment were often cited as the cause of an initial opening, whether it was feeling guilty about participating in an operation or a sense of disillusionment with the tactics of bombings more generally. These emotions, however, were not sufficient to cause disengagement without other factors reinforcing them over time. This raises the question of why. For operatives and followers, feelings of disillusionment may be counterbalanced by peer pressure and the obligation to obey one's seniors (*sami'na wa atho'na*); that duty to obey may have caused them to temporarily bury their misgivings or stopped them from speaking out against an action. For several, the obligation to "hear" the order and "obey" it came when Hambali relayed Osama bin Laden's declaration of war to his subordinates and subsequently proceeded to plan attacks to carry it out. One Afghan veteran who attended meetings where early bombings were planned described the discussions that took place and the pressures upon him to go along:

> In Afghanistan, there were four *ustads*—Sheikh [*Syeikh*] Abdullah Azzam, Sheikh Abu Thoiban, Sheikh Abu Burhan, and Sheikh Abdul Rosyid Sayyaf. These ulama gave us input, and they encouraged us. Ustad Abu Sayyaf did not emphasize bombings or jihad. He called to us students, "Later, when you return to Indonesia, you have to pursue gentle *dakwah* in your communities." So when Hambali plotted [violent] actions based on the fatwa by Osama bin Laden, we tried to respond with the opinions of Abu Thoiban, Abu Sayyaf, and Abu Burhan. I believed that the Osama fatwa was suitable to legitimate fields of war like Afghanistan, Iraq, Palestine, or Ambon or Poso. In my view, if we could have taken into account and implemented fatwas by those *ustads* [Abu Thoiban, Abu Burhan, Abu Sayyaf], there would have been no problem. However, I was part of Ustad Hambali's group. And we were moving already [i.e., planning attacks]. I could not reject [the bin Laden fatwa]. I was then instructed [to participate] in several incidents, the incidents that sent me to jail. There, I contemplated whether my action was correct. But when the act was in progress, I could not speak against it because of *sami'na wa atho'na*.[7]

He would put his misgivings to the side, participating in the 2003 Marriott bombing as part of the logistics team tasked with procuring the explosives. While he disapproved of the tactics and the fatwa legitimating them, he did not turn away because he felt bound by the call to hear and obey his seniors.

In another instance, "Reza," a mid-level operative from Mujahidin KOMPAK, was ordered to assassinate a prominent figure from Nahdlatul Ulama (NU), an Islamic mass organization in Indonesia with a membership close to fifty million. Since Reza came from a Muhammadiyah family,[8] he was concerned that if he killed the NU figure, it would be taken as a child of Muhammadiyah killing a child of NU. He faced a clash of identities in this instance, where his identity as a Muhammadiyah youth conflicted with his identity as a Mujahidin KOMPAK member in good standing. "At the time, I thought this was bigger than just killing someone. I seriously disagreed with [the] tactics. However, as a subordinate, I did what I was told. This was *sami'na wa atho'na* [I hear and I obey].[9] He was arrested before he could carry out the assassination. In both instances, a period of incarceration ignited in these men a period of reflection, which would lead to disengagement in the former case but not in the latter. In short, disillusionment is indeed a key part of the disengagement process in many instances, but if other factors don't reinforce it, feelings of disappointment and misgivings about tactics and targets may not be sufficient to lead to disengagement.

Alongside disillusionment, rational assessment also contributed to the decision to disengage. Thirty of those interviewed cited rational assessment. This manifested in one of two ways. In former conflict zones like Poso, it was an evaluation of the changing context. Poso was now peaceful, and it had been more than a decade since the last attack by a Christian militia. There was no longer a need to use violence. JI and Mujahidin KOMPAK members on Java tended to apply cost-benefit logic with several lines of reasoning. First, most interviewees pointed to general public revulsion with the bombings and expressed the general sentiment that ongoing bombings would be "counterproductive" to the interests of JI and Muslims in general. Alongside this view, it was often mentioned that bombings against civilian targets were a violation of the Quran's rules governing the conduct of war. Thus, there were religious "costs" involved with taking such a step. Especially among Afghan veterans, the view was that bombings and other such indiscriminate attacks aimed at civilians was "forbidden according to Islam."[10]

Ali Fauzi, a Mujahidin KOMPAK member who had been a trainer at JI's Camp Hudaibiyah in Mindanao and fought in Poso, explained,

> We understood that Ambon and Poso were real jihads at that time because [in those regions], there was conflict and war. In Ambon and Poso, there was a Muslim side and a Christian side. Then, friends moved the conflict to a safe area. To Jakarta and Bali where there was no conflict. The real enemy did not exist there. I did not agree with their plan to enlarge the conflict from Ambon and Poso to Bali and Jakarta. My friends' reasoning was that Americans were killing civilians. But even if Americans were killing civilians, it does not mean that we Muslims may also kill civilians. There is a code of ethics in Islam. In jihad, there is *adab al-jihad*, a proper way to do jihad, a proper way to wage war. So the explosions that occurred in Bali and in Jakarta are, in my view, counterproductive to the jihad in Indonesia.[11]

Another, an Afghan veteran asserted,

> The violence had to be stopped. The Muslim community needs a clear understanding of jihad. If we do it wrong [i.e., violate the

Quran's rules of war], then we contribute to a misunderstanding of
jihad, and then the jihad will go badly.[12]

Another line of reasoning asserted that JI was too weak to employ
violence in pursuit of an Islamic state in Indonesia at this time. Each
time they carried out a terror action, they were discovered and captured. All the training, all the weapons collected, went for naught,
because certain individuals were too caught up in shortsighted strategies and lost sight of the long-term goal.[13] Thus, while terror actions
might have their time and place in the future, when the group had
adequately prepared, for now the losses from such actions would
exceed the benefits.[14] Related to that, it was often noted, especially
by Afghan veterans who tended to be of an older generation, that
violent actions had adverse consequences for the network's *dakwah*
activities. For example, because of increased surveillance as a result
of actions like the Bali bombing, it was difficult for their leaders to
hold mass prayers to spread their message to the public.[15]

These arguments regarding public disapproval, the strength of
the enemy, the costs outweighing the benefits, and the indiscriminate nature of the violence resulting in civilian deaths were part of
a larger JI narrative espoused by many in the leadership, including
former amirs Abu Rusdan and Zarkasih.[16] While some jihadists
within JI and Mujahidin KOMPAK circles arrived at these conclusions via discussions with their seniors, others did so independently via reflection. Particularly after 2007, however, the reality
that these arguments were being disseminated within JI circles and
from JI leaders may have been reassuring to those who questioned
the utility of violence or felt a sense of disillusionment with a particular target or their role in an attack.

The third factor, and arguably the most important for facilitating reintegration, is the building of an alternative social network of

supportive friends, family members, and mentors. As an ex-Ambon fighter explains, "Someone's frame of thinking often depends on the frame of thinking of friends around him or her. One's change in thinking or ideology is strongly influenced by who their friends are."[17] Given how important social ties are to membership in JI and its affiliates and given the extent of overlapping kin and quasi-kin relationships, it is not surprising that the development of new ties would be important to disengagement and eventual reintegration. If individuals are going to distance themselves from their prior social network, it helps to have developed a new group of friends, mentors, and colleagues.

The most frequently mentioned type of relationship was new friendships, which was mentioned by a total of thirty-one individuals. The building of new friendships offered new narratives for perceiving the "enemy," refocused priorities from jihad and/or revenge killing back toward one's family, and challenged previously held views. One Afghan veteran who participated in the bombing of the Philippine ambassador's residence and fought in Poso explained how his friendship with a Christian leader, Rev. Rinaldy Damanik, in prison, prompted a rethinking:

> [My change in thinking] was the result of reflection and experience. We were mixed with the priest, Damanik, in prison. We were close to him in prison, so why not outside? It got me thinking. [In prison], we ate together. We played sports together. Damanik had his master's degree. We had graduated from the Afghan [Mujahidin] academy, which was not regarded [as legitimate] by the government. We needed to learn from an academic, someone with a master's degree. I heard something good from Damanik. He said, "We should promote that we have no problems with each other, a peace campaign, as soon as we are released." However, my friends responded negatively. They said, "Why are you so close to Damanik,

the mastermind of the Poso conflict?" I responded, "Let bygones be bygones. There is now law enforcement."[18]

In this instance, the friendship formed resulted in the humanization of the other side. Former antagonists interacted with each other, ate together, played sports together, and formed a friendship. They shared the experience of being in prison. It didn't make sense to continue the conflict in prison; their sentences would only be extended. Thus, the friendship and the reality of the situation led to a cost-benefit assessment that it was better to put the Poso conflict behind them. Now that law enforcement had been upgraded and Muslims could be duly protected by the security forces, they could move on.

In other instances, new friendships can highlight inconsistencies in behavior and serve to underscore the contradiction between rhetoric and reality. For one former member of the Subur cell, a group that aided bombing mastermind Noordin M. Top following his excommunication/departure from JI, befriending Daniel, the only Christian in the prison, offered him a new perspective on his seniors when he witnessed them treating the Christian unjustly. He explains,

> There was dangdut music playing loudly, and my three seniors did not like dangdut. They committed a mistake in their *dakwah*. They named Daniel as a suspect, and at night they threw stones toward his room. I was angry. Daniel could not possibly have been the one blaring the dangdut; he didn't like dangdut. They didn't know that; only I knew that. So I said to my friends, the terrorists, "It is not possible for Daniel to be the one playing the music. I know Daniel. Stop throwing rocks at his cell." But they showed him no justice. They weren't just. Although Daniel is a Christian, they still need to practice Islamic law fully. When you suspect an individual of doing something, you must investigate first. They did not investigate before they acted.[19]

This incident, combined with other inconsistencies in behavior, alienated this particular militant from his seniors. They represented a starting point where he began to ask different sorts of questions and to see things through different lenses.

> I changed. I saw people. I saw individuals. I stopped being so quick to label someone as an infidel or a hypocrite. I didn't change my core Islamic principles, but I changed in how I saw leaders. I will be more careful in choosing my friends. I will be more careful in choosing my teachers.[20]

Business relationships had a small impact in reinforcing behavioral disengagement, because they encouraged interaction with bureaucrats, Christians, Chinese, and secular Muslims. As JI and Mujahidin KOMPAK members often reinforce relations with business ties, new business ties often present a way out, a way to reinforce a change in priorities.[21] For "Amru," a JI member who trained and fought under JI leader Abu Tholut in Mindanao and later served time in prison when weapons were found hidden in his home, working at a restaurant forced him "to interact with people in buying and selling, to converse with people."[22] In 2010, he was offered the opportunity to train in Aceh as part of a cross-jihadi organizational initiative of members of Jemaah Islamiyah, Mujahidin KOMPAK, Ring Banten, Jemaah Anshorut Tauhid, and other groups. He thought about it, but he ultimately refused, because doing so would jeopardize everything he had built.[23] There is, however, a limit to the power of business ties vis-à-vis friendships and familial ties. Business ties can be driven by pragmatic considerations rather than interpersonal connections. For example, several Poso jihadis pointed out that Christians and Chinese dominate the local economy; if they shunned those individuals, they would have no business. Moreover, if the business fails, the ties may not be sustainable.

Another important relationship was familial. Support from parents and spouses was a key reinforcing factor in disengagement. One Tanah Runtuh member, from the first generation of recruits, explains how his wife, whom he loved deeply, prevailed on him to quit.

> What pressured me most is my wife. She said, "In the future, if there is a major outbreak of unrest, you go ahead [and fight]. But now, look to us first. The family must be taken care of." In the end, I focused on my family.[24]

Another Tanah Runtuh member, who had participated in the bombing of the Tentena marketplace, reflected on his parents' emotional appeal and how it persuaded him to turn himself in to the police.

> I escaped [Tanah Runtuh] on January twenty-second [during the Densus raids]. Soon after, I went home. My parents asked me to surrender. Initially, I refused. It was impossible to surrender myself to the enemy. My parents were crying. It was the first time I saw my father cry. I followed the wishes of my parents.[25]

In this instance, the reaction of his father shook him out of the mental model under which he had been operating and reoriented his thoughts toward another set of values—those of obeying his parents. The converse, however, is also true. In each case where an individual remained radical and committed to participation in further actions, he named parental support as a key factor in his thinking. One JI member, whose father told him repeatedly that he hoped he would die a martyr, was dedicated to finding any opportunity for jihad that would enable him to fulfill his father's request. He now has a good job. He is focused on his family. Ultimately, he stated at a meeting in 2016, he sees himself as on a break until an opportunity to fight in a jihad presents itself. In another instance, "Yuda," a hit-squad member from Tanah Runtuh, professed to have the full support of his parents in conducting revenge attacks. He was one of the very few who held fast to the hard-line position, and after escaping prison in 2013 he fled to the hills to join Mujahidin Indonesia Timor (MIT) and immediately took up arms again.

Familial socialization can also serve this function in a quieter way. If children were raised by parents to be tolerant, open-minded, and to have a firm understanding of Islam, then those ideas may eventually reassert themselves in the consciousness of the particular youth. One Ambon fighter came from a Muhammadiyah family and had attended Muhammadiyah Quran study groups prior to the outbreak of the Ambon conflict. He explained that he initially went to Ambon seeking to participate in humanitarian relief actions. However, he quickly fell in with JI and KOMPAK notables and, angered by the anti-Muslim violence taking place in Ambon, soon participated in attacks against Christian targets. After his arrest, when he began to reflect on the Ambon conflict and his role in it, he soon reverted to the religious thinking of his upbringing. He explained, "In general, Muslims want their daily activities to be based in sharia, but this does not have to be violent. It can be accomplished without war through *dakwah*. That thinking was part of my background. . . . I am not a radical person"[26]

Personal and professional priority shifts away from seeking opportunities for jihad or participation in terror actions and instead toward pursuing further education, seeking gainful employment, putting food on the table, paying the bills, and focusing on one's family were also an important part of twenty-eight disengagement narratives. Together with building an alternative social network, priority shifts were key to reintegration. The two factors often appeared together and reinforced each other. For example, two of those interviewed had been encouraged to pursue their bachelor's and master's degrees by new friends from outside the jihadi circle. For both these individuals, the opportunity to go back to school led to the development of new opportunities, new relationships, and new perspectives. Ali Fauzi, the younger half brother of Bali bombers Muchlas, Amrozi, and Ali Imron, was encouraged by Ali Imron and Noor Huda Ismail, the founder of the Institute for International Peace Building, to pursue a college education. He went on to attend Muhammadiyah University in Malang, where the books he read and the interactions with other students opened his mind to new ways of thinking. Because of these experiences, he contends that he now identifies more with the Muhammadiyah community than his former community and feels accepted by them.[27]

However, a priority shift may be far simpler. In a jihadist group, an individual's top priority is his duty to that group. That reality can chafe against personal wishes. As one Afghan veteran who had since left JI to become a Salafi explained, "I was not there when my son was born because I was on duty to pick up Abu Bakar Ba'asyir from the airport. For three days, I could not see [my son]. That would never happen among the Salafi. When a child is born, the father must be there."[28] In iterated interviews with Tanah Runtuh members in the years following their release from prison, each came to prioritize "*cari makanan*," or putting food on the table for the family, as more important than pursuing further opportunities to mount revenge attacks against Christian targets; given that Poso was peaceful, these men said they would "relax" and "enjoy life." One Tanah Runtuh member of the elite paramilitary unit, the

Team of Ten, had found fulfillment in his new job as a civil servant. He noted that he would not join MIT because it would "alienate his new friends."[29] In fact, he had since become estranged from his circle in the jihadi community and confided that his only association with Tanah Runtuh in 2015 was helping Haji Adnan Arsal by cutting through bureaucratic red tape or assisting him via small grants to his schools. Another Team of Ten member, following his wife's pleas that he disengage, since the circumstances and conditions had changed, resumed the profession he held prior to the outbreak of the conflict. He was a respected builder, known for his expertise in working with both wood and stone. Thus, we can ascertain that his priorities did not necessarily shift away from jihad but *back* to his first loves—his family and his profession.

Interaction Effects

In disengagement narratives, there is considerable overlap between factors, creating an interaction effect where one factor builds upon another. Oftentimes, these center, in one form or another, on various types of new relationships reinforcing a personal or professional priority shift. For example, when Noor Huda Ismail encouraged specific disengaging jihadis to further their education or aided them in obtaining employment, the establishment of a new relationship facilitated a priority shift. In yet another version of the interaction effect, disillusionment is often expressed in a combination of rational cost-benefit terms and deeply emotional language. In these instances, the realization of the profound costs of terror actions may create a profound sense of disappointment and the feeling of being let down by leaders who should have been firmer or wiser. The reverse of that relationship can also be true. One's nagging discomfort with bombings or with his role in bombings may lead to a cost-benefit reassessment of the costs of such actions on the whole. The interaction between the emotional and rational assessments may serve to push disengagement forward and come to facilitate priority shifts as one becomes more convinced of the need to cease the use of violence or to leave the movement altogether and construct a post-jihad life.

The importance of interaction effects and their gradual evolution can be understood clearly by examining the case of "Agus," a former member of Mujahidin KOMPAK currently serving a life sentence in an East Java prison.

Agus's story begins following his graduation from high school, when he moved to Jakarta to look for work. He had joined in activities of the underground group the Indonesian Islamic State (NII) in high school, but when he departed his hometown, he left the group, finding them too idealistic for his tastes. After a short stint with a construction firm in Tasikmalaya, where he quickly became dismayed by the rampant corruption, he moved to Jakarta and lived in his uncle's house.

His neighbor was the key to his entry into a social circle that would later become Mujahidin KOMPAK, a paramilitary group loosely connected to Dewan Dakwah Islamiyah Indonesia (DDII, or Indonesian Islamic Propagation Assembly). The more he conversed with his neighbor, Ustad Muzayin Abdul Wahhab, a member of DDII, the more he realized he had met a kindred spirit. While the goals of NII seemed impractical, DDII focused on doing *dakwah* (Islamic propagation) in order to educate Muslims about Islam. He became Ustad Muzayin's student, together with another young Muslim who would also later feature prominently in KOMPAK, Abdullah Sunata. In time, he met Ustad Muzayin's brother Aris Munandar, who would go on to become KOMPAK's senior commander. In May 1998, Suharto resigned, and in December

1998, communal violence between Muslims and Christians broke out in Ambon. Because of his relationships with Aris Munandar and Ustad Muzayin, Agus soon found himself at the center of the aid response efforts.

> When the conflict broke out in Ambon, I wanted to help my brothers and sisters there. The media stories told of Muslims slaughtered as they performed the morning prayers and Muslims evicted from their homes during Idul Fitri holidays. DDII dispatched some members to verify whether these stories were true and found that they were. Then, KOMPAK [their humanitarian relief arm] mobilized to provide aid, collecting clothing and food to be delivered there. I participated as a volunteer. Initially, I was just a volunteer. I felt pity for my brothers and sisters in Ambon.
>
> I met Pak Aris Munandar at my neighbor's house, and he told me he was going to depart for Ambon in October to deliver aid. If I would like to come along, I was free to join them.
>
> I arrived in Ambon and was welcomed by the sound of bombs. At the time, the conflict between Muslims and Christians was at its peak. I was scared because I had never confronted such a situation before. I only saw it in movies. . . . However, the bombs in Ambon were real. I could not even walk from the Muslim areas of the city to the non-Muslim areas without bodyguards.

As part of the first group of KOMPAK relief workers-cum-fighters dispatched, Agus helped set up the KOMPAK office in Ambon that would also be used as a base for JI fighters. At first, he did relief work and guard duty. According to Agus,

> we were expected to safeguard the area. When we were asked to help execute counterattacks, we worked hand in hand with them. At first, I felt scared, but as time went on . . . I began to feel brave because I knew the doctrine that those who die in battle will be rewarded in heaven. Those who die as martyrs defending religion would be rewarded with the right to marry seventy angels, and they

don't really die. They are still alive and hover around heaven, flying everywhere. So I didn't feel scared anymore. I was brave. I was no longer afraid to die.

In his description of his reasons for joining the jihad, it is important to note that piety was not the foremost motivator. Instead, Agus was affected by what he had heard and read about the conditions of the Muslim community there.[30] Thus, he joined the jihad largely for reasons of solidarity with his fellow Muslims. At the time, he had assumed he would be providing aid, but he found himself swept up in the atmosphere of the conflict and joined in the fighting. Yet, as part of the fighting, he drew strength from his faith. He regularly attended *taklim*, and what he learned in them about his life after martyrdom increased his level of enthusiasm. He would take a direct role in the 2000 raid of the Police Mobile Brigade (Brimbob) barracks at Tantui, where jihadists from Maluku and outside Maluku made off with some one thousand guns.[31]

Agus's experiences in jihad were not confined to Maluku. In 2000, he spent eight months fighting in the jihad in Poso as part of Mujahidin KOMPAK, together with Ali Fauzi and other Javanese Mujahidin KOMPAK members. In 2001, he went for further weapons training at an MILF training camp, although he did not fight, because the MILF was in peace talks at the time with the government. Subsequently, he returned to Ambon and participated in a series of village raids in November 2001. Then he went back to Java, taking a break to marry and start a family. In 2005, a friend approached him with the opportunity to join another action, and he returned to the field. The plan was to attack the Christian hamlet of Loki village on Ceram Island. However, first they needed to eliminate the Brimbob police guard post.

[In 2005], a friend of mine from Ceram came to Ambon asking for help. He said the Christians in the hamlet were making trouble and provoking anxiety among the Muslims. We left Ambon for Ceram. We attacked the hamlet, which was guarded by Brimbob personnel. One of them shot at me. I shot at him. I fled Ceram with my other colleagues. Five Brimbob members were killed in the attack. Three of us were shot. I was [later] arrested in Ambon.

The decision to join the attack on the Brimbob post at Loki would change the course of his life. To that point, he had participated in jihad activities during a period of communal violence. However, the Loki attack took place three years after the Malino accords, and police officers had been killed. The police were determined to discover the identity of the "jihad group" in Ambon. Agus and his co-conspirators were arrested; Agus was sentenced to life in prison for killing the police officer. Over the next three years, he was moved from prison to prison, first in Maluku, the province where Ambon and Ceram are located, and then to a prison on Java. It was during his time in prison there that he began to reflect.

[When I attacked the Brimbob post] I felt brave. I felt I was right. I felt strong. I had been in excellent physical condition. But after I was in prison, I started to think about what I had done. Those Brimbob members who died were also Muslim. I began to question whether I had done the right thing. I [began] to feel guilty. At one point, I tried to convince myself that I did not attack them. I tried to convince myself that I had instead attacked the Christians who had attacked us. But I failed to convince myself because those who died in the attack were [in point of fact] Muslims. How had the situation ended like this? I was confused. Then, I let it flow. I discussed it with friends who were arrested along with me. One said we should have no doubts. We had done the right thing. We were defending our brothers and sisters in Ambon. I just kept quiet, but in my heart, I was questioning whether our past actions were right.

Agus had begun to feel unease with his own actions, for they had resulted in the deaths of Muslims; this was his starting point. Then, after he reflected on the costs of actions such as indiscriminate killings and bombings for the Indonesian Muslim community, he came to the conclusion that the costs were indeed far too great.

> If bombings don't benefit Muslims, why do it? It's better to stop it. Instead of bringing benefits to Muslims, these events bring losses to Muslims. For example, Muslims being perceived as being fond of killing people at random, it's not good.

In jail in Maluku, he came to know several Christian fighters.

> They were jailed for possession of bombs and weapons. We were sharing the same fate, so we felt no animosity toward one another. We shared our experiences and our stories. We did sports together. From them and from others that visited the prison, members of the police, the officials from the Dewan Perwakilan Rakyat [DPR, the People's Representative Assembly] and others, I learned about the many interests in Ambon. There were political interests [involved]. People [who wanted] to assume official posts. I began to think about whether this was purely a religious conflict. The more information that I learned, the more I began to understand what had really been happening in Ambon. I concluded that Ambon had been a political fight, a fight over projects, a fight for winning government posts, and I regretted the reality. For those of us who fought, we could only see the houses that were destroyed.

Thus, for Agus, three factors ignited the process that would eventually lead to his disengagement. First, once in prison, as he reflected on his own actions, after going through a period of denial, he felt a growing sense of unease with his past choices. In the process, he assessed the costs of participation in the Loki attacks. He came to feel disappointed in his past choices. Third, as he became more acquainted with individuals outside his jihadi circle—fighters from Christian militias—he came to see they all shared a similar fate. Discussing shared experiences with them humanized the other side for him. Additionally, from the police and government officials, he came to have a greater understanding of the root causes of the conflict, which reinforced his sense of disillusionment with his own involvement in the violence. This was not a religious conflict; it was a political conflict masquerading as a religious one. Additionally, conversations with Nasir Abas and Noor Huda Ismail reinforced this thinking. Nasir Abas, the former commander of Mantiqi 3 of Jemaah Islamiyah, who now works with the police on disengagement efforts, met with him on four occasions since his imprisonment.

> He shared his opinion, and I thought it was good. [He said] that jihad must be the correct jihad. It cannot be done at random. Jihad must be done in the manner exhibited by the Prophet Mohammad. Jihad is not bombing here and there at random. The right jihad is a civilized jihad. The right jihad does not kill women, does not kill parents, does not damage churches or other places of worship. I [had] known these things for a long time, but perhaps I had been carried away by the situation, so my earlier knowledge was forgotten. Now, I understand.

Noor Huda Ismail and Taufik Andrie, the founders of the Institute for International Peace Building, reached out to Agus following his arrival on Java, eschewing ideological discussions in favor of simply treating him with kindness. "Noor Huda helped me through his actions and opened my eyes. He did not think 'you're a terrorist; you're not deserving of help.' He cared about me, even though I was labeled as a terrorist." When Search for Common Ground held a conflict management training session, Noor Huda and Taufik recommended Agus, which in turn exposed him to new models for understanding and resolving conflict (see chapter 8 for more details).

Thus, interacting with individuals from outside the jihadi circle and developing friendships and acquaintances with individuals brought new perspectives, new ways of thinking, and brought to mind lessons once learned and temporarily forgotten. These interactions are key to understanding Agus's shift in perspective. They reinforce one another, each offering new opportunities for communication and new information on the Ambon conflict.

The interaction effect among disillusionment, cost-benefit analysis, and new relationships with individuals outside the jihadi circle led Agus to disengage from violence. Physically, it was impossible for him to do otherwise; he was in prison serving a life sentence. Intellectually, however, his personal reflections, his feelings of disillusionment and the cost-benefit calculations that emerged as a result of his conversations and interactions with individuals outside the jihadi circle, led to a shift within Agus. He began to think about reintegrating and building a life outside the Indonesian jihadi movement. He explained that this need to build a new life took shape the first time he saw his mother following his arrest. "She just cried, and I cried." He revealed to me in 2012 that his parents were already old. He felt guilty for having abandoned them. His father passed away during his time in prison. Thus, it is important to him, after he leaves prison, to reintegrate successfully for her. When he is released, he says, he will return to his hometown and become a farmer. It is perhaps lucky for him that he has served much of his sentence at Porong prison, for he has been able to take advantage of the prison's life-skills training program in farming and animal husbandry.

The Conditionality of Disengagement

It is important to note that disengagement for the majority of those interviewed came with conditions. For many Java-based jihadis, the conditions they set for further involvement in terror or jihad actions made the likelihood of future participation quite slim. These conditions can legitimate disengagement, if they set a high bar to reengagement. They can point to a reassessment of previously held views on jihad, shifting from an offensive and defensive model to a purely defensive one, or reaffirming support for a purely defensive one. Individuals can thereby rationalize disengagement— they have become more open, yes, but they have remained true to their principles. If the bar is lower, however, the conditionality can also be used to shift back into one's former life.

The most common response among those interviewed, especially those who fought in the Soviet-Afghan War, was to state they would again take up arms if Indonesia was invaded by China, Russia, or the United States. This statement is grounded in the standard understanding of jihad as an inherently defensive action—protecting your country from invaders—and very much in line with the decision-making calculus of Afghan veterans who went to fight in Afghanistan to help the Afghans rid their country of the Soviet invaders. Should they find themselves facing an invading army, as unlikely as that would ever be, they would again choose to fight. In the words of Anas, whose narrative is highlighted in chapter 3, "For *jihad qital*, when we are attacked, we are obliged to defend ourselves. So if another country attacks Indonesia, I am ready. But if they do not attack, I will focus on my family."[32] Agus concurred with this assessment, stating that "if Indonesia was invaded by a foreign power, I would join *jihad qital*." When prompted, he went on to explain, "If conflict in Ambon or Poso broke out again, I would have to study its causes. Even then, I would probably still just give aid or join in the peace effort."

Other jihadists sought to follow in the footsteps of the Afghan veterans and Moro veterans. Abdul Rauf, a Ring Banten member who fought with the Islamic State of Iraq and Syria (ISIS) until his death in Ramadi, Iraq, in 2014, was most characteristic of this line of thinking when he asserted in early 2012, "When there is conflict, we have to help Muslims being oppressed. I'll be ready to help oppressed Muslims anywhere." Interestingly, his decision to go to Syria and fight in Iraq was completely in accordance with the conditions he placed on his further engagement. While he believed that Indonesia was not a legitimate venue for jihad, he still expressed the desire to participate in jihad to help the cause of oppressed Muslims.[33]

In the realm of the probable, several stated they would go to Ambon again, if the conflict there was reignited. Moreover, all Poso jihadis interviewed contended that if the Christians attacked them, they would again take up arms to defend their neighborhoods.[34] One jihadi from the first group of Tanah Runtuh recruits explained what conditionality meant to him: "It is like this. If I have to face the red militia [the Christian fighters from Tentena], I am ready."[35] If that attack never came, or until that time, however, he was happy to continue his life as a civil servant.[36] This is again grounded in the understanding of jihad as a defensive act, either defending one's community from invasion or protecting those under attack.

Recidivism: Reza

In light of the conditionality of disengagement and the variation in degrees of commitment to disengagement, there is always the likelihood that individuals feeling a sense of disillusionment or assessing costs and benefits while in prison may choose to reengage when they leave prison, if certain incentives or tempting opportunities present themselves. A person may drift back into the jihadist community by helping friends in more and more concrete ways. This is especially true in instances where someone has not begun to reintegrate into society by building an alternative social network, or if attempts to "go legit" fail because someone cannot make ends meet. This section will highlight Reza.

Reza was born and raised in Lampung, Sumatra, the youngest of five brothers. He did not come from a radical family. Of all his siblings, only he joined a radical group. Only he participated in jihad. He attended a Muhammadiyah high school and was raised with a view of himself as a Muhammadiyah youth, an identity that may have become less significant as he entered the jihadi community but one that remained a part of how he saw himself. One of his grandfathers was in the Indonesian military, so he grew up around guns and always liked playing with guns. This affinity for guns features prominently in his narrative, but its origins lay not in his life as a jihadi; he remembers that even in elementary school he liked guns.

Upon finishing high school, he left home for Jakarta, preferring to find work rather than continue further schooling, and settled in the Cipayung area of East Jakarta. He met Abdullah Sunata and Agus, two prominent figures in Mujahidin KOMPAK, at the Nurul Hidayat mosque, and they discussed the conflict in Ambon. Reza quickly became enamored with the idea of going to fight as a real jihadi in Ambon and went for a ten-month tour with Mujahidin KOMPAK. He explains that joining with Mujahidin KOMPAK was simply a means to an end. "I was not recruited into KOMPAK. I was not interested in joining or not joining Mujahidin KOMPAK. I just wanted to help my brothers and sisters in Ambon."

Initially, he was tasked with bringing in medicine and other aid to help the Muslim victims. However, in time, he was trained as a soldier. Following the conclusion of his Ambon experience, he was sent to Poso, for only two months this time, assigned to bring weapons, medicine, and supplies to his comrades at Kayamanya. He returned to Jakarta in 2002, and following the first Bali bombing, he was given the responsibility of bringing Dulmatin, Umar Patek, Uceng, Sawad, and other Bali bombing participants to the Philippines to link up with the Abu Sayyaf group, whose leaders had vowed to give them refuge in their territory. He had, in years past, developed a reputation as a capable go-between who knew the routes to Poso and to the Philippines by which one had the least risk of being detected. He spent two years in Abu Sayyaf territory in the Philippines and contends

> this was the best time of my life. I was fighting in a real jihad against a legitimate enemy, the army of the Philippines. During these years, I was interacting with al Qaeda, with Algerians and Kuwaitis. I felt that Allah was watching over me and protecting me. I believed the actions I was doing were the highest form of good deeds to Allah. Yes, I felt scared, but I also felt brave and happy.

In 2004, Abdullah Sunata called Reza back to Jakarta to again serve as a go-between, to transport people to the Philippines and Poso. Together with Anas, whose narrative is featured in chapter 3, he was also tasked to procure the detonator cords and TNT for the Australian embassy bombing. He contends that by this time, "I understood that bombings were wrong, but I was a soldier." *Sami'na wa atho'na* (I hear and I obey) trumped his independent reasoning. Both he and Anas were arrested in 2005 for their roles in the bombings. While Anas would disengage and reintegrate into society, Reza would not. He served six years in prison before being released in 2011.

Upon his release he came to a conclusion. "When I walked out of jail, I decided I was done with Mujahidin KOMPAK." This might lead one to believe that he had in fact disengaged. However, he was just tired of taking orders from Sunata. "I still saw myself as part of the jihadi community. I wanted to help many jihadi groups and not just be part of KOMPAK." His shift away from Sunata has its logic, since Sunata had ordered him to assist in the Australian embassy bombing and to assassinate a prominent NU figure. He disagreed with both these actions but felt bound by his status as a soldier. It was only luck that he had been arrested before he carried out the assassination, which he feared held significant consequences, as he was a child of the rival Muhammadiyah organization.

In the year following his release, he made a halfhearted attempt at reintegration, trying his hand at several businesses, but he was unable to make enough money. However, he never attempted to widen his social ties to include friends from outside the jihadi community or construct an alternative social network. By 2013, he had started a new business as a gun runner, selling compressed-air-powered sport guns and other firearms. This drew him more solidly back into the orbit of various radical groups. He sold guns to anti-Shia militias and to the militias acting in support of the Rohingya people of Burma. The police bought his guns as a form of monitoring his activities. Interestingly, he contends he was tasked by them to participate in a gun buyback program in Ambon, where he collected guns from former fighters and turned them back to the government. Thus, the security apparatus was well aware of his activities. However, in 2013 he also sold guns to a friend, who sold them to a middleman, who subsequently sold them to Mujahidin Indonesia Timur (MIT), a prominent jihadi group based in the mountains around Poso. For that, he was arrested again.

Reza served twenty-four months and was released in June 2015. When asked what he intended to do upon his release, he declared with a happy-go-lucky grin, "I am going to sell guns again. I like guns." Then he became more serious. "I am going to try not to sell them to MIT this time." By September 2015, he had resumed selling guns and made no attempt to hide this from anyone looking. His Facebook profile picture shows him holding a gun positioned as if to shoot. Visiting with Reza and Anas (see chapter 3) in 2016, I confronted him regarding the riskiness of his Facebook page if he intended to ever make a life for himself outside of gun running. He contended that he was doing it for his own protection. There were hard-liners from pro-ISIS groups who were threatening him; he put up such a page to show he was unafraid. At the time of that meeting in 2016, he had begun working as a motorcycle driver for Gojek, an Uber-like service for motorcycle taxis, occasionally making TV appearances as an ex-jihadi, and Anas was pressuring him to go back to school. He responded that he did not know how to obtain funds or where to begin. I suggested, since he came from a Muhammadiyah family, that he look to a Muhammadiyah university. As of our last conversation, he was giving shooting lessons and working for Uber.

The case of Reza offers important insights for government officials and security officials working in counterterrorism and addressing questions of recidivism. While some jihadists may choose to reengage because they are captivated by the idea of joining ISIS and fighting in what they view as a "legitimate jihad," Reza did so because he lacked the capacity and connections to make a viable living via a nonviolent trade. His areas of expertise were in guns and in transporting people via clandestine routes around Indonesia and to the Philippines. Given that he had such an affinity for guns since childhood, coming from what some might call "a gun family," the fact that he took up selling sport guns and firearms to make a living is not surprising. Selling guns, however, did not enable him to expand his social network, nor did he build relationships beyond his jihadi circle. If he expanded any social network, it was within the radical community, from Mujahidin KOMPAK to anti-Shia, pro-Rohingya, and MIT affiliates. Thus, he was pulled deeper in. After spending two more years in prison, he was cavalier about taking up gun running again. He would try to be more careful about whom he sold to, but he seemed content with his position at the fringes of many radical movements. A year after his release, however, he seemed to be taking the first steps toward another path, but it is hard to make ends meet as an Uber driver. It looks like Reza could, with proper assistance and training from a professional development program, go legit, possibly return to school for a degree, and reintegrate.

THERE ARE FOUR factors that, in conjunction with one another, have been driving the disengagement of jihadists from Jemaah Islamiyah and its affiliates. Feelings of disappointment with the movement's tactics, leaders, and, to a lesser extent, hard-liners; rational assessment; relationships outside the jihadi circle, including friends, parents, and mentors; and changing personal and professional priorities are most responsible for disengagement. Oftentimes, disillusionment or cost-benefit analysis leads the jihadist to begin to question his participation in the movement or whether a particular action was justified. Over time, other factors may build on that initial opening, creating an interaction effect, where the jihadist increasingly begins to focus on reintegration—creating a post-jihad life built on new priorities and relationships.

The most common interaction effect was when disillusionment and rational assessment are reinforced by the building of new relationships and social networks. Those relationships, in turn, encourage the individual to pursue new educational and employment opportunities and validate the desire to spend more time with family. The realization that the cost of continued participation exceeds the benefits may come into play at various points in the process, as well as familial pressure. Such a complex pathway was far more common among those jihadists who chose to disengage by leaving the movement or going inactive, compared to those who disengaged but remain involved in the movement and its activities. The latter had simpler interaction effects, often centered on cost-benefit assessments.

The converse is also true. Even among those who go through the reflective rational assessment process or feel some semblance of disillusionment, if they do not build an alternative social network or at least a social network of in-group friends supportive of disengagement, if they do not shift their priorities toward professional development and family, they are more likely to reengage, if the right opportunity emerges.

Finally, in each instance, the individuals placed conditions on disengagement. Often these conditions were grounded on a classic understanding of jihad as a defensive action. For example, if Indonesia were invaded, it would be necessary to take up arms to defend the country. If communal violence re-ignited in Ambon or Poso, it would be necessary to defend Muslims living there. Rather than disengage, others actively sought out new jihad experiences elsewhere, wanting to find a way to travel to Iraq or Syria and join the fight. We would be remiss if we dismissed disengagement because it came with conditions. While a low bar of conditionality can lead an individual to reengage—those truly seeking a jihad experience rather than just talking about it will most likely find one if they try hard enough—it is not the same with a high bar. Indonesia is not likely to be invaded by another country. The building of new relationships and networks, the pursuit of an education, and the obtaining of gainful employment create barriers to future jihad participation as well; those who rejoin their former life may lose all they had built.

3

Anas

I never changed; they changed.

—*"Anas"*

A nas's story begins in high school. His parents decided to enroll him in a local madrasa for high school. He had been quite a brawler in junior high school, frequently clashing with other boys in the class above him. Thinking that enrollment in a conservative Islamic school would straighten out their son, perhaps force him to quit smoking, and encourage his religious devotion, they pushed him to go to a madrasa rather than the public high school in his hometown.

While a student at the school, he was invited by friends to join two study circles, both of which would have a significant impact on his religious and personal development. First, a classmate invited him to join a Salafi study group that met on Friday, the Muslim Sabbath. That same year, he was also recruited into Tarbiyah, an insular, religiously conservative movement that drew upon Muslim Brotherhood teachings and methods of organizing.[1] Anas describes his participation in both groups.

> I participated in the Salafi study session on Fridays, when there was no school, while I also participated in a daily Tarbiyah movement

study group on school days. My activities with the boys in Tarbiyah taught me how to organize and run an organization. They taught me how to participate in campus activities. The Salafi group appealed to me more because of their spirit for jihad. The study of jihad in Tarbiyah circles lacked substance, so I had to find another place to learn about jihad. I appreciated the strengths of both groups, however, and remained in both groups. The Salafi study group nurtured my spirit for jihad. Tarbiyah's study groups cultivated a spirit of unity and brotherhood among Muslims. I appreciated that my senior in Tarbiyah would travel twenty kilometers [from his house to mine] daily just to see if I performed the early morning *subuh* prayer.

In time, I followed a friend from the Salafi group into a Madrasa Diniyah [after-school Quran study], run by Jemaah Islamiyah, although I did not realize it at the time. After about a year studying in the Madrasa Diniyah, I began to realize that they were likely not Salafis. Their books, Syed Qutb, Abdullah Azzam, Mawdudi, indicated that they were likely something else.

Until the Ambon riots in 1999, Anas continued to participate in both communities: the Jemaah and Tarbiyah. With the fall of the Suharto dictatorship in May 1998, the Tarbiyah movement formed a political party, the Justice Party (PK), to take advantage of the newly open political scene, and Anas became a PK cadre. When the conflict in Ambon broke out, however, Anas's superiors within the JI community insisted he choose between PK and their Jemaah. After initially rejecting the contention that he needed to "choose" one because he learned complementary information and skills from both, he chose JI, believing it to be more "perfect." At that time, however, he did not realize he was part of a transnational terrorist group; he did not realize it till shortly before the Bali bombing, when Muchlas would tell him that the Jemaah he was part of was actually Jemaah Islamiyah.

Anas's ease at joining movements, making friends and mentors, and seeing the complementary nature of differing groups would

be an asset to him during his time in Jemaah Islamiyah and Mujahidin KOMPAK and remains a continued strength. He quickly
would befriend key members of both JI and Mujahidin KOMPAK,
notably Zulkarnaen and Aris Munandar, who would become his
mentors. When JI began sending fighters to Ambon, Anas wanted
to go, but he was prevented from doing so because he was "still
learning." He had not gone through military training. As part of
the preaching division, he was instructed to leave the fighting to
the soldiers. Disgruntled, he then approached Aris Munandar,
with whom he had studied Islam, and asked to go as part of Mujahidin KOMPAK, his humanitarian relief-cum-paramilitary outfit.
By 1999, he had started university, so he waited until the semester
break, biding his time by joining the KOMPAK media unit and
writing articles about events in Ambon. In 2000, he departed with
the second batch of Mujahidin KOMPAK fighters for a three-
month tour of Ambon, bringing books and medical supplies with
him. He was not the only JI member to go to Ambon via Mujahidin KOMPAK; Mujahidin KOMPAK set up operations on the
ground more quickly than JI. Thus, impatient JI members often
went as part of Mujahidin KOMPAK, resulting in overlapping
membership between the groups. Although departing with Mujahidin KOMPAK, Anas took his military training with JI, learning
basics like map reading and field engineering. While he primarily
participated in humanitarian aid operations, he also joined in several attacks. By his own characterization, he was "very young, only
nineteen," and "highly spirited."

Reflecting on his participation in jihad in Ambon, Anas says it
was a profoundly spiritual experience.

> Before I departed for Ambon, I was taught about jihad: what
> it is, what the rewards would be if I did it. When I was there,

I became addicted to it. We have to be aware that jihad is addictive. Some people say that violence is like opium. First, our adrenaline spikes. Second, when we are doing jihad, we are worshipping Allah to the utmost. If you're at the top, what more do you need to do? Even when we ate, we knew that we would be rewarded in heaven. When we were observing the movements of our enemies, we knew the angels were taking note of what we were doing and that we would be rewarded in heaven. It was beautiful.

He went back and forth to Ambon five more times on short trips to bring supplies, but otherwise he focused on his studies and his activities with the media wing. During this period, he stayed at a safe house and mixed with people quite high in the pro-bombing wing of JI, including Muchlas, who finally got around to giving him the oath to formally join Jemaah Islamiyah. Dr. Azhari, the master bomb maker, stayed there; Dulmatin and Imam Samudra came and went. He watched as people in the safe house built bombs. While he was focusing largely on his activities in the media wing, on occasion he participated in work on electrical circuitry, thinking they were building bombs for Ambon. More and more people turned up throughout the month. They worked all through Ramadan. Shortly thereafter, in October 2002, two bombs exploded at Paddy's Bar and the Sari Club in Bali. Dulmatin, whose wife had just given birth, appeared with a newly slaughtered goat, and everyone celebrated, eating goat curry. Then everyone was ordered to leave the house. As they cleared out, Anas began to consider the possibility that these activities and visitors had been part of the Bali bombing.

In 2003, he continued at university, finishing a diploma in information technology prior to his arrest. He reflected on the events leading to his arrest:

I took leave from the university and went to Jakarta to involve myself in jihad activities again. I was sent to Ambon in 2004. There I met someone named Ubaid. He said that someone wanted to meet me; it turned out to be the professor [Dr. Azhari] and Noordin M. Top, who I knew from my time in the house. I asked permission of my supervisor in Mujahidin KOMPAK, Abdullah Sunata, to meet with them, and he granted me permission. Ubaid asked me for ten kilograms of TNT. When we met, I gave over the TNT. He, in turn, told me he had new materials, a CD about the struggle, articles written by Abdul Qodai, Abdul Aziz, and new translations from al Maqdisi regarding divisions among Muslims. I read all the articles after I arrived in Ambon and gave them to the fighters.

When I arrived in Ambon, I expected to see Muslims and Christians fighting, but instead I found something new. We were planning to attack a police post and take the weapons. We did a training on Ceram island. As the training was in progress, I thought I was being followed by an intelligence officer and decided to go back to Jakarta. Then, the Kunningan bombing occurred. I told Sunata I was going to do my public service at university and would be unavailable for the semester. I left Jakarta for Yogya. I stayed away from the other jihadis except for some small editing jobs. I felt safe. I was asked to edit a video of the Ceram training as a gift to a visiting sheikh. I was on my way to Jakarta to deliver it when I was arrested for my role in the Kunningan bombing. I had provided the TNT to Ubeid, you see.

The shift in Anas's thinking began prior to his arrest. He explains that, sometime in 2004 and 2005, he began to start thinking differently from his more hard-line friends. He maintains, "I never changed; they changed." He explains:

Before I was arrested, I started to have different thoughts from my [JI] friends. Especially Syaifuddin, who was a kind of spiritual adviser; he was able to memorize the Quran in forty-four days. After returning from Saudi Arabia, he started to teach people different teachings. For example, [he said] if we do *sholat* [prayer] behind a civil servant or a Prosperous Justice Party [PKS] person who turns out to be *kafir* [an infidel], we are not allowed to pray behind him. [He said] when we do prayer in areas dominated by civil servants, we are not allowed to participate in prayers led by civil servants. I disagreed bluntly. I told Syaifuddin that it would be difficult for us to congregate for prayer, for example Friday prayers. I realized the teaching was getting more right wing. I was OK with some matters related to it, but for other matters, we need to assess. . . . Let's take PKS, for example, I cannot label them as infidels. I saw the effect of the movement. As Aris Munandar said, Islam does not consist of a single institution. PKS exists, and we have to take into account the positive side of PKS. It was things like this that led me to view this radical turn as something that would lead to a negative impact.

In this instance, the growing extremism of his friends, beyond what Anas thought was practical, sparked a rethinking for him. He was becoming increasingly disillusioned by his friends' hard-line views, particularly Syaifuddin, whom he considered a mentor and a spiritual adviser. He believed that dogmatic stances such as "don't pray near such-and-such type of person" would not work in the reality of congregational prayers and that such ideas more generally promoted division among Muslims rather than encourage unity. When his friends included PKS among the infidels, this also alienated Anas. He knew the party and the Tarbiyah movement that undergirded it and respected their positive attributes. Even if he had left the movement, he still saw himself as part of it. When he challenged Syaifuddin on these points, Syaifuddin refused to "mingle" with him any longer. That divergence in opinion was all it took to end the friendship. Seeing various Islamist groups as having their own complementary roles in bringing about an Islamic society and Islamic state, Anas was uncomfortable with such a narrow perspective.

Another such moment came when he discussed al Maqdisi's teachings about believers and disbelievers with the *takfiri* ideologue Aman Abdurrahman. "I argued with Abdurrahman and his supporters regarding their stipulations, and over the course of the debate I showed them that, by their logic, all their lawyers were unbelievers. I was laughing and happy. But I was done. I could not convince them. Hence, I quit."

Around the same time, he also began to regret some of his own actions, particularly spreading the works of *takfiri* Islamic ideologues and theologians who were responsible for dividing the Muslim community. He cited an example of creating an app for Aman Abdurrahman to deliver sermons via cell phone.

From an intellectual standpoint, Anas was willing to engage in dialogue with the hard-liners rather than isolate himself from them. However, he would not assist them again. "If you want to have a conversation with me, it's fine. If you don't want to, that's fine too. They should be comfortable with me to the point that they don't disturb me and I won't disturb them."

Anas maintained his relationships with those JI members whom he admired and trusted. However, he also sought out new relationships and reestablished old ones. He was surprised in prison to find that his friends from childhood and friends from PKS visited him. No one from JI did. The knowledge that he had the support of his friends, despite what he had done, despite the fact he was now in prison, let him know who his real friends were. In perhaps a surprising turn, while in prison, he would form a friendship with Suryadharma, then the head of Densus 88, the police antiterror team. Anas explains how his friendship with Suryadharma opened him up to new possibilities.

Pak Surya has a high social empathy. He acted as a facilitator because he pointed out things that I needed to do. There were still

many things in Islam that I could do. For example, we visited scavengers and orphans and blind people. JI people never did that. We
have to admit the people who often visited scavengers were PKS
people.

Noticing the promise in Anas, Suryadharma also permitted him
to work on a second bachelor's degree, which was quite an ex-
traordinary show of trust, given that Anas was permitted to leave
prison for classes, so long as he returned when they were over.
Anas suspects that his parents prevailed on Suryadharma to let
their son proceed with his studies. During Anas's time in prison,
Suryadharma also facilitated his marriage. Following his release
from prison in 2010, Anas began to work for Suryadharma as a
personal assistant for a year. As a result of these relationships and
experiences, Anas's priorities shifted, which further reinforced his
decision to disengage.

> My priority is to dedicate myself to society through social works. I
> assist in activities to benefit society, for example the management
> of Islamic micro-finance that is being done by Pak Suryadharma; I
> like that kind of activity. I also run goat breeding. My target is to in-
> clude people in running it so that they will be positively affected by
> the activity. Just like Muhammad Yunus, doing social works for the
> community. But Muhammad Yunus only gives out funds. I would
> also like to help people developing their businesses.

In 2011, Anas left Suryadharma's employ to chart a new professional course with his wife, and from that he has not waivered. He
has built new friendships, friends who know nothing of his prior
life, friends who do not know he fought in Ambon, or had ever
been a member of Jemaah Islamiyah or KOMPAK. Both he and
his wife have achieved a measure of professional success. This has
made Anas fiercely protective of his privacy. He fears losing it all,

should his new friends and colleagues learn about his past. Thus, he asked me not to disclose his new profession.

In Anas's disengagement, cost-benefit analysis and disappointment mingle closely. His disillusionment initially centered on the increasingly hard-line views of friends, who in adopting a *takfiri* mentality were responsible for dividing the Muslim community, and the instances in which he, as a member, contributed to fostering those divisions. However, Anas also had become deeply disappointed with the tactical errors made by the bombers. When we met for the first time shortly after his release from prison in 2010, Anas repeatedly lamented what he saw as a "lust for jihad" overtaking rational analysis on timing, location, condition, and target in ascertaining whether an action was legitimate and appropriate or not. In his view, this lack of robust assessment had adverse implications for JI. He contended that the Christmas Eve bombings, the Philippine ambassador bombing, the JW Marriott Hotel bombing, and the Marriott and Ritz-Carlton bombings as "not quite right. There were too many local victims. In war, we need to make friends, not create enemies." He explained his point of view:

> If we create more enemies, we will be attacked here. Society will not like us. It will lead to difficulties for us. We have to have a scale of priority, who needs to be killed, who does not need to be killed. Let me give an example, and please forgive my rough language. If I say, in my opinion, there are people involved in democracy and because they are involved in democracy, they are infidels and need to be killed, it will spark a problem. After we kill them, it could generate accusations from others. How do we explain it to the public? The public will ask why a Muslim killed another Muslim. So when we do terror actions, we need to look at where an action is supposed to be done and what will be the impact of the bombing.

Our friends sometimes ignore norms, and I don't like that. Bombs cannot be put anywhere they like. They should have detonated bombs in the right place and time and on the right target. For example, if you hate Densus 88, why did you kill traffic police as well, who are not on the same level with them? I don't like that. If you hate them, you kill them not because you hate them only but because al Quran orders you to kill them because they oppress Muslims, for example. . . . Look at the latest actions in which they put cyanide poison in food in the police canteen. It was not right. Not only police but also ordinary people ate there. I don't like this kind of action.

As a result of these failures, JI as an organization has suffered.

We have sacrificed a lot of stuff. Our equipment has been confiscated. A huge amount of money has been confiscated. Manpower has been wasted. How many dozens of years would we need to collect that same number of weapons, that same amount of money? How could we create a new Dulmatin?

Anas chose to disengage via departure from JI, rationalizing that since Muchlas, the leader who inducted him, was now dead, the oath was no longer binding. However, he has not chosen to sever ties with like-minded JI members. Instead, he continues to view himself as a "JI sympathizer" and remains friendly with those in JI who shared his viewpoint, which is, in fact, widely held.

It is highly unlikely that Anas would ever reengage; if he did so, he would lose everything he had built. Even if the Ambon or Poso conflict broke out again, he would

first look at the cause of the conflict. Some conflicts are intentionally made. Others break out by accident but are inflamed by intelligence services [or other outside actors]. So there should first be a survey team. I would need to look at the conflict. Then I would need to assess which group I would join. The situation is different now compared with the past. In the past, I knew exactly who was sitting next to me. I lived with them, slept with them, and I knew their character. I knew some of them ever since I was a youth. We fought for the same cause. Today's activists lack information on who is standing next to them because they never went through jihad education. Since we don't know who our friends are and who our enemies are, things would likely turn out different. Regardless, I will not be one to fall into a trap. I will not become bait. I don't want to involve myself in any sort of situation like that.

Anas's story is especially notable because it highlights the ways in which the factors motivating disengagement reinforce one another. Anas became intensely disillusioned with those who would divide the Muslim community and label others as *kafir*. In his view, there are various forces in the Muslim community, and each has its own role to play in bringing about a just society. This was a view he had held prior to joining JI, throughout his tenure in JI, and continues to hold today. Anas also realizes that he has been party to spreading this division among Muslims, bringing CDs and articles to Ambon that speak to the unbelievers among Muslims and making an app for Aman Abdurrahman allowing him to spread his divisive rhetoric via cell phone sermon from his prison cell. He feels regretful. Because of his disillusionment with his newly hard-line former friends and with his own role, he began to distance himself from those espousing these intolerant hard-line views. Around the same time, he began to assess the costs and benefits of terror actions. Anas may have played only a small role in one attack, but he was a very social person, and he knew everyone. He had gone through a year and a half of indoctrination. He saw JI build itself as a network, accumulate weapons and funds, and then he saw how some, moving too quickly to leapfrog to bombings, before the network was ready to take on the state, had led it to lose everything, its manpower, its weapons, its resources. Its best minds were dead, on the run, or in prison. The costs of such actions had surely exceeded any benefits. Moreover, he was intensely disillusioned with the current generation of local jihadists, some of whom did not even have a basic knowledge of prayer.

The friendship with Suryadharma in prison provided external reinforcement to what had to that point been an internal reflective process. It introduced new thinking about how different types of people can do good deeds to benefit the Islamic community and provided him the opportunities to further his education. This facilitated a change in priorities. All the while, his feelings of disillusionment and disappointment with tactics and targets of terror actions were increasing. Anas's disengagement narrative is built around these four factors, where disillusionment and cost-benefit analysis, the feeling that the friends in his community had moved too far to the right of him and in doing so had damaged their network and their aspirations, form the interaction effect. The building of new relationships, facilitating a priority shift, constitutes a second important interaction effect, reinforcing the first.

Today, Anas has achieved a measure of professional and personal success. He has become a father. He enjoys his work. He is fiercely devoted to ensuring that his past does not negatively impact his family. He fears it would stigmatize him and even his wife by association. Over dinner at his house in 2015, he declared, "The *ikhwan* are ready to reintegrate into society, but society is not ready for us."

4

B.R.

When we were together, we thought with one mind.
When we were separated, we began to think for
ourselves again.

—*B.R.*

B.R.'s story begins with a news broadcast he saw while living in Palu in early 2000. The Poso conflict had begun two years earlier, characterized at that point by sporadic bouts of tit-for-tat gang warfare between Muslim and Christian gangs. B.R. had been apprenticing in a print shop prior to the conflict. He enjoyed the work, having an artistic flair, and learned to screen T-shirts and print banners. In his spare time, he played guitar and sang with a local singing group. He had Christian friends, mostly fellow musicians, as well as a Christian uncle.

The broadcast relayed the news that Laskar Jihad, the militia wing of the Salafi al Sunna Communication Forum, had entered Ambon to provide assistance. Ambon was also facing communal violence.

Major conflict had broken out in Ambon. I watched television and saw a story of Laskar Jihad members entering Ambon. I told myself that I wanted to be like them. I wanted to join Laskar Jihad. One of my friends and I even made an agreement that if we heard word of Laskar Jihad entering Poso, we would notify each other and join them together.

Whereas communal violence in Ambon received international attention, there was very little focus on Poso, and thus, very little assistance was forthcoming. In April 2000 there were a series of clashes between Muslims and Christians, and B.R. joined in. He participated in an attack on a police post in a Christian village. Subsequently, a subsection of Christian community formed "red militias" and sought to mount revenge attacks on the Muslim community or "provocateurs," as they referred to them.[1] They made small-scale forays into Muslim-dominated areas of the city, including Moengko and Kayamanya, and killed three people. Violent incidents took place around the city.[2] Clashes moved closer to B.R.'s home, just across the river in Gebangrejo. B.R.'s mother fled the city. The attacks culminated in the Walisongo massacre on May 28, 2000, where the Christian militiamen attacked a mosque and Islamic boarding school at Walisongo, torturing and killing the men and sexually assaulting some of the women. David McRae, author of *A Few Poorly Organized Men: Interreligious Violence in Poso, Indonesia*, estimates that at least one hundred were killed over the course of the four-day attack. Neighboring Sintuwulemba village was razed. Attacks also occurred during the same period in the north of the city. The two weeks of clashes left most Muslims in Poso with a strong desire for revenge. Local Muslim clerics were calling for jihad.[3]

The Walisongo massacre galvanized B.R. While he personally had not lost close family in the fighting, he saw the broader costs of war. He saw that Muslims living in largely Christian areas had been displaced, their homes burned. An uncle by marriage had disappeared. After Walisongo, B.R. wanted revenge and sought a means to carry out that revenge against the Christian fighters.

In the weeks following the Walisongo massacre, trainers and fighters from Jemaah Islamiyah and Mujahidin KOMPAK began arriving in Poso, at the request of Haji Adnan Arsal, a local Muslim cleric. The young Muslims generally had great respect for Arsal, who had stayed behind when many other Muslim clerics had fled. Arsal ran an Islamic boarding school in the Tanah Runtuh neighborhood, an area that, according to B.R., was one of the major entry points for Christian "red" militiamen. Muslim youth had already been gathering in Tanah Runtuh to prevent the red militia from slipping into Poso. However, activities escalated with the influx of the Java-based fighters. The earliest arrivals from Mujahidin KOMPAK and JI had experience in fighting, either in Afghanistan or Mindanao, and they took it upon themselves to indoctrinate the youths and offer military training to those who showed promise. Tanah Runtuh as a group began to take greater shape, with Arsal's compound as a focal point for activities.

Laskar Jihad would not arrive until later that year. As a result, while B.R. initially sought out Laskar Jihad, he encountered the trainers sent by Jemaah Islamiyah. He describes his initial encounters with the "*ustads* from Java":

> When I went back to Poso to visit my family, I went to the mosque to pray. On one occasion there was a mass prayer, and from it I learned things I never knew before, namely about jihad and how it is an obligation incumbent on every Muslim. I continued to participate in their mass prayers and other religious activities. After a little while, I was informed there would be a training for those who were actively participating in the religious gatherings. I was ready. I had a feeling that this was what I was looking for. We congregated at the An Nur mosque and left for a week of field training in Wekuli village. After I participated in the training, the brothers from Java

became heroes to me. Their presence boosted my morale. I was selected to be a part of the Team of Ten. I am not sure why. The order
came from one of my instructors. When we returned home, they
administered the oath to us.

After the training program, we Muslims no longer waited for
the Christians to attack first. We no longer ran away. We took the
offense. We attacked the Christian villages.

B.R. was part of the first batch of recruits and was selected to be
part of the elite paramilitary wing of Tanah Runtuh, the Team of
Ten; he would subsequently help to train others recruited in the
second and third batches in how to fight. When they raided Christian villages, he was one of the commanders.

Just when B.R. and his friends felt they had gained an upper
hand in the fighting, however, in December 2001, Susilo Bambang Yudhoyono, then coordinating minister for security affairs,
Yusuf Kalla, then coordinating minister for people's welfare, and
religious leaders from both sides promulgated the Malino peace
accords. The security forces also increased their presence, in order
to maintain calm. B.R. found the Malino accords unfair. "We had
just started to exact our vengeance, and then suddenly the parties
all signed the Malino accords. The accords failed to mention the
"sixteen names"—the additional perpetrators believed to be responsible for the Walisongo massacre. For eight months following
the signing of the accords, there was relative calm. The members
of the Tanah Runtuh militia took their objections to Malino to
the government officials and their elders. Not receiving a response,
however, they began to attack villages. According to B.R., the most
significant such attacks he participated in as part of Tanah Runtuh
were the 2002 attack on Mayumba village and the 2004 attack on
Kawende village. According to B.R., he and his friends were grateful that the "people from Java" came to help out. However, he did

not suspect they were members of Jemaah Islamiyah until he saw coverage of the October 2002 Bali bombing on television and realized he knew several of the people being arrested.

> One of them called himself Abu Asap. There were three Ahmeds. [After seeing the TV footage], I started to think that they were involved in the JI terror network. Then, because I was taught and nurtured by them, I realized that I too was automatically part of the network. But I did not care about it. I looked at the context. I looked at Poso as a local situation. I participated in the conflict to protect our brothers and sisters in Poso.

B.R. was happy during that time, practicing jihad with his fellow members of the Team of Ten in Tanah Runtuh because he had friends with "similar views and similar understandings on what we were supposed to do."

In May 2004, he was called on to participate in an action that would disrupt that comfort and prompt the first inklings of a shift in thinking for him. He explains that by 2004, Poso was already safe. The last bout of fighting had been in August 2002. However, a subgroup of fighters from Tanah Runtuh had formed a hit squad and decided to continue exacting revenge against mostly Christian targets. B.R. had been designated as a team leader, a middle management position within the organizational structure. Under the supervision of Hasanuddin, JI's point man in Poso, and Haris, one of the Tanah Runtuh leaders, members of the group would select targets and coordinate with other members to carry out attacks. It was a decentralized process. B.R. found that he was selected by Haris for one of his operations, the assassination of a prosecutor. B.R. explains his feelings:

> I went to Palu and met Haris, my paramilitary commander, who had masterminded that [particular] attack. I followed the

prosecutor for three days to learn his routines. . . . We learned he
was going to participate in a Christian mass prayer. We followed
him, and when he was on his way home from church, we shot him,
Haris with an M-16 rifle and me with a revolver. He was brought to
the hospital and died there.

When I went back to Poso, I felt . . . because I did it. This was
different than other attacks. I was not being attacked and having to
defend myself. This was not that.

I did not know why this prosecutor became a target. Why him?
He was not from Poso. He had not bothered our brothers and sisters in Poso. But then, Haris explained that he had disparaged the
sharia in one of the court sessions. [As a result,] he became a target.

Actually, I had been trying to get out of participating in the attack. In order to avoid joining the action, I said, "Ris, I have no
weapon." However, he said there was a weapon, he had stored it. If
he had said there was no weapon, I could have returned home to
Poso. I tried to avoid it, but he said he had a weapon.

B.R. had begun to feel a sense of unease. He may not have felt guilt
per se, but something did not feel right to him about the action.
Whereas he understood attacking a village as one force attacking
another during a time of war, Poso had been peaceful for two years
at the time of the assassination. This action differed because he was
attacking not a police post or a village of Christians, but a single
individual who had not participated in the conflict. He even tried
to come up with an excuse to go home, by "forgetting" to bring a
weapon, but when he learned they were providing him with a gun,
he did not have the strength of his convictions to outright refuse to
do it. He was not ready, at that point, to break with his friends. He
expressed no disagreement, bound by a sense of solidarity. When
he returned home, he continued to congregate with his Tanah
Runtuh friends and join in mass prayers. In some small way, however, he was shaken, and he began to assess costs and benefits of

specific actions and become more selective in his involvement. He joined the raid on Kawende village and a robbery. He planned a terror attack on a flag ceremony but aborted it at the last minute, citing the target location as being too heavily guarded. When he was unwittingly brought into the Tentena market bombing, being tasked to bring a tube container from Palu to Poso after being told it was for stove parts for a friend's *gorengan* (fried snacks) business, he was dismayed. "Had I know what it was for, I would have found a way not to deliver it." However, the dominant influence in his life at the time were his friends in Tanah Runtuh, and they continued to shape his perspective.

The next year, in 2005, he came upon the office of the Central Sulawesi Group for the Struggle for Women's Equality, a human rights group that had opened an office in his neighborhood. He began coming to the office, sitting in the back and listening to their conversations. There, he met A.B. and Masykur, two of the activists on staff. By his own account, he says he went there to learn information.

> A.B.'s office was close to my house. I visited the office often. It was always packed with people. It was a good place for me to find information about what was going on in Palu and Tentena and other places without actually having to go there. People who lived in those areas came to the office to share information. From there, I could draw conclusions about what was happening in those places.

Over the next year and a half, B.R. became a regular feature around the office. In time, A.B. recruited him as a volunteer and slowly began to break down his walls and gain his confidence. "I chose B.R.," she says, "first because he was a good communicator":

> He could interact with anyone from any segment of society. Second, he was unemployed, and I thought it was better for him to

be employed, empowered, and useful rather than doing nothing or things that were not clear. Third, he was already helping out at the office a lot, guarding, helping with office work. It was good for us [to have him and his friends around] because it made us feel safe. The project took longer than expected, so we had to stay. I had to document the mysterious bombings and killings and shootings, and that required fieldwork. When I had to go into the field, I asked B.R. to take me everywhere because I knew he was someone with guts to face whatever would happen, but he was also a local who knew the places we wanted to go. . . . I kept asking him about the events. Who did this? But he would always say he did not know or did not understand. Perhaps because he saw me as an outsider. [At the same time], he was a good friend for discussions, and there were a lot of office programs. I would tell him about what we did, our peace mission, about things like inequality, human rights, poverty, and more. I often told him that everything that happened in [Poso], it was the state that bore responsibility. The state failed to provide security and enable the people to treat each other with tolerance.

During the year and a half that A.B. was in Poso working on the project, she and her colleagues became an alternative community for B.R., a place for him to hear views outside of the Tanah Runtuh groupthink. While he continued to congregate with his hardline friends in Tanah Runtuh, and their shared perspective on the conflict remained dominant in his thinking, his new friends were slowly introducing him to a new point of view on how to understand the Poso conflict, and he was coming to trust them. A.B. and B.R.'s mother were also growing close. A.B. said, "I would often visit with B.R.'s mother. I would stay at her house. She considered me like another daughter."

A.B. had long been trying to break through B.R.'s mistrust. She knew it was likely that he was involved in some of the attacks that had been going on in Poso; to what extent, she was unsure. In 2006, however, she was given an early copy of the newest most-wanted list (DPO), which included the names of twenty-nine Poso jihadists; B.R.'s name was among them. With that, she directly broached the subject with B.R., warning him that the DPO list would soon be released on TV and print media, and they would come looking for him. Via telephone, she advised him to either surrender himself or flee, but that before he decided, they needed to talk in person.

> When we finally met, he honestly told me everything he had done. Every accusation toward him was true. I asked why he didn't tell me sooner, and he said that he did not fully trust me. I asked him all my questions. Were you involved in the robbery? [He responded] I was involved in keeping [the proceeds]. Were you involved in the mutilation of the schoolgirls? [He responded] "No. I did not take part. I did not agree with that act. In war, women and children must be protected." Like that. He told me everything. I told him I was willing to help him. I was going to go back to Palu and would discuss the matter with friends that I could trust.

By the time A.B. arrived in Palu, however, the security apparatus had released its most-wanted list on television. B.R. had grabbed his things, stuffed them into a backpack, and joined others at a house on Jalan Pulau Jawa near Tanah Runtuh. The next morning, the police distributed pamphlets around Poso with the names and photos of the Tanah Runtuh young men on the most-wanted list, as well as the crimes they had been accused of. Even when approached by the Tanah Runtuh spiritual leader Haji Adnan Arsal, whom they respected, B.R. and his friends were adamant they would not surrender. They fueled each other's convictions. "When we were sought by the police, we did not surrender because we knew it was not permitted for us to do so. However, there was no solution. Since we didn't want to surrender, it was better to leave Poso." B.R. went into hiding.

Three months later, on January 11, 2007, Densus 88, the police counterterror team, raided Tanah Runtuh. The night before, coincidentally, B.R. had sneaked back into Poso and slept at his mother's house. In the morning, his brother woke him, saying there was fighting at Gebangrejo near Tanah Runtuh. He washed and dressed and prepared to go, but his mother stopped him. B.R. described the exchange: "'You are not allowed to go,' she said. 'If you go, it is not you who will die. I will die.'" He explained, "She cried, and I could not go." B.R. obeyed his mother, and that act likely changed the course of his life. He realized that if he ran toward the shooting and something happened to him, his mother would lose her son. He knew how much his mother loved him. This would have destroyed her. Therefore, he stayed behind and did not participate in the two-day shootout. He was not one of the sixteen dead. He was not among the dozen arrested on that day. When he learned of the death of his good friend Dedy Parsan, he cried. Adnan Arsal gathered together the remaining Tanah Runtuh boys and advised them to *hijrah* (migrate). For B.R., this was a decision point. He could flee with his Tanah Runtuh friends, or accept help from A.B. and her circle. While he considered the former, he ultimately chose the latter.

After hearing about the raid, A.B., her husband, and a few of their friends offered B.R. a place to hide. They saw promise in B.R., trusted him, and thought they could get through to him. By the next raid on January 22, he was safe in Palu, watching the events on the news. To pass the time, he read constantly. A.B. and her friends kept him well supplied with their bulletins, as well as books, which were centered on issues pertaining to the people and had a decidedly leftist bent. He conversed with A.B., her husband, and their activist friends, and these discussions began to influence his views on the Poso conflict.

> I observed she saw the conflict in Poso was not one between Muslims and Christians. The conflict became protracted, and each side took revenge. She gave me input sometimes. I mingled with the group and learned from them. I have a lot of gratitude to A.B. for that.

Every few weeks, he was shifted to a different house. At A.B.'s home, he busied himself with creative tasks. He built a gazebo to keep them cool; made dozens of toy guns out of paper, black paint, and sticks; and painted huge renditions of SpongeBob and Spiderman on the external walls of their compound to amuse A.B.'s young son. He went out rarely, only locally to the market or to play a pickup game of soccer in the neighborhood. He kept his head down.

Thus, the initial process of disengagement began for B.R. with his participation in an action that did not quite feel right. The target seemed improper, as the victim had played no role in the Poso conflict. He was not a fighter; he was a civilian. Moreover, the timing was off; Poso had been peaceful for two years. When B.R. returned home after the action and resumed his normal activities, a powerful set of new relationships, his friendship with A.B., her husband, and the other activists, offered him a new narrative for perceiving "the enemy." In time, he began to understand the Poso conflict from a wider perspective. It helped greatly that his mother was a constant voice, pointing to an alternative path away from violence. In time, he came to trust his new friends in the activist community, especially when A.B., her husband, and their friends agreed to hide him from the authorities. It took going into hiding, away from his old friends in Tanah Runtuh, and having the opportunity to talk with A.B. and her husband, as well as to read and reflect, that led him to develop his own views on the permissibility of violence, his willingness to use violence, and his own place in Tanah Runtuh.

All during this time, B.R. still considered himself a member of Tanah Runtuh. What changed over time was that he realized the Poso conflict was far more complicated than he had originally thought; it was not a religious battle where all Christians were the enemy. That realization brought about others. The more time that went by in Poso without a Christian attack, the more it seemed that the conflict had ended; the time for violence was over. Ultimately, he says, in 2007 or 2008, he came to the conclusion that too many innocent people had died as a result of their actions. "People became victims who should not have become victims. I began to think seriously about who was truly an enemy." When I asked B.R. what was the most important factor, he said it was his mother, first, and then A.B.

After two years in hiding, he began to consider surrendering to the authorities. Behaviorally, he had long since disengaged. Intellectually, he had arrived at a point that justified that disengagement. The next step for him was to accept the consequences of his participation in the attack against the prosecutor. Key individuals and moments in his process of surrender reinforced his decision to disengage. First, he had the support of A.B. and her husband, who encouraged him to think about his future and his family. They had been pushing him to surrender for some time. The stress on all the involved activists, but especially A.B., was taking its toll. In hiding him, many friends and family members had been put at risk. Then, he sneaked home to tell his mother and seek her blessing. Her warm and sincere reply provided crucial moral support for a decision for which he had mixed feelings. She told him, "I have waited so long for you to surrender yourself. I always prayed for it. I was praying for your heart to be moved." She explained to me that while he was in hiding, she didn't know where he was.[4]

> I prayed that Allah would open up my son's door so he would sur-
> render to the police. Every night, I prayed like that. When he was in
> hiding and the police would come to my house, I would tell them,
> "Do not shoot him. I know him. He will change. He will come
> back."

Haji Adnan Arsal agreed to act as a go-between and then proceeded to negotiate B.R.'s surrender to the police, exacting two
important promises: first that A.B. and her friends would not
be charged for harboring him (he was adamant on that point),
and second that he would not be tortured. He had long resisted
surrendering, fearing that his friends would judge him harshly
for doing so, and that he would face torture at the hands of the
police. "I imagined my toes would be pinned under a desk that
they pressed on from above." However, he explained that when
he finally walked into the provincial police headquarters, the police chief instructed his subordinates, "B.R. has come in peace,
so we have to accept him with peace." At that point, he said, "I
felt safe." Initially, he was held in a cell connected to police headquarters; A.B. visited him regularly during this time, fearing he
could sink into depression; often she brought her son, who had
come to see B.R. as family. She also kept him well supplied with
reading material.

B.R. continued to worry about his friends in Tanah Runtuh and
their judgment of him. Nasir Abas, the former head of Jemaah Islamiyah's Mantiqi 3 training division, who now works with Densus 88 to assist in disengagement, visited B.R. in prison shortly

after his surrender and reinforced his decision to surrender by providing moral support. B.R. explained,

> I saw that my friends still did not want to surrender, while I surrendered. I knew my friends were displeased with me. I shared my concerns with Nasir Abas when he visited me in prison. He reassured me, "Don't think about that. Before you surrendered to the police, there were many others who surrendered themselves." He boosted my spirit.

At the trial, he met the wife of the prosecutor he had killed. He apologized to her, and she forgave him. Seeing her cry at the trial also made an impact on him. "I began to see what we had done from a human point of view, when his wife wept." He received an eight-and-a-half-year sentence and served six years of it, before his release in April 2015.

Disengagement for B.R., as for all Tanah Runtuh members, is conditional on Poso remaining peaceful. If the Christian militias attack again, B.R. and his friends in Tanah Runtuh will fight to defend their communities. However, B.R. has no intention of looking for a fight, in contrast to other Tanah Runtuh fighters who have joined Mujahidin Indonesia Timor (East Indonesia Holy Warriors) headed by a former member of Tanah Runtuh, Santoso. While some Tanah Runtuh members believed that Christians would eventually attack and characterized their disengagement more as a break until the fighting resumed, B.R. was firm in his desire to avoid future violence. He explained, "When I was in Poso, it was not clear who was my enemy. I started to narrow down my definition of an enemy. I came up with this: if I am not disturbed, I will not fight. In the past, my friends and I were active in pursuing my enemies. However, now I think that if I am not attacked, I will not attack. I will not pursue."

When B.R. was released in April 2015, he began to focus on reintegrating into society. He moved back home to Bonesompe to live with his mother and siblings. He was pleased to find himself embraced and welcomed home by his former bandmates. They got the band back together and quickly picked up a gig twice a week at a local club. This adds another layer of alternative social network. A.B. and her friends provided an important social network for facilitating disengagement, but they now live in Palu, five hours from Poso. However, his childhood friends from the neighborhood welcomed him home and back into their circle—the circle of friends he had been part of before the outbreak of the communal conflict. While he still spends time with his jihadi friends, who congregate regularly at a spot in the neighborhood of Kayamanya, he contends that he is just visiting (*silaturrahim*). He also will attend the occasional charity event at Tanah Runtuh or mass prayer around Ramadan. However, he spends far more time with his bandmates and his family.

B.R.'s main focus is opening a print shop, specializing in banners, stamps, and T-shirt screening, in time for the next round of elections. He has picked out the land and drafted a business plan and a budget. He is looking for seed capital. His business partner is one of his bandmates. He contends he is very happy. "I can meet my mother, my family, anyone now. No more hiding. I can work now."

5

Ali Imron

We need to admit when we do wrong things so that it
can be a lesson for others.

—*Ali Imron*

Ali Imron's story begins in junior high school. He had been pestering his parents to let him follow his elder brother, Ali Gufron (alias Muchlas), to Ngruki, the hard-line Islamic boarding school established by JI founders Abdullah Sungkar and Abu Bakar Ba'asyir. His parents were reluctant; they wanted to keep their youngest son close to home. When he was about to start high school, his brother, Jabir, also a student at Ngruki, died in a mountain-climbing expedition. "It was pure miscalculation by those leading the climb. They had too much faith, but not enough work and preparation was done. So they emphasized faith only and ran out of everything while high up on the mountain. There was a storm and heavy fog. They had no water, no nothing. They were told to descend, they had nothing left, and all were lost."[1] In the aftermath of this family tragedy, his parents finally relented and decided to let Ali Imron go to Ngruki. Ali Imron found, perhaps to his surprise, that he was not comfortable with Ngruki's strict regulations and "extreme lessons."[2] He was horribly homesick; after just one month there, he feigned an illness so his parents would come for him.³ He returned home and began attending school at a local madrasa run by Muhammadiyah. He admits, during this time, he focused far more on hanging out and driving cars than his studies. "I stayed out late roaming around in cars and just hung out. . . . That's all. It was just a teenage phase. I figured as long as I could pass the final exams, I would be OK."⁴

During exam week, however, he attended an Islamic discussion organized by KAMMI, the successor to the Tarbiyah movement and precursor to the Justice Party (PK). The discussion dealt with the topic of oppressed Muslims in the world, notably the cause of Palestine and the jihad taking place in Afghanistan. This was a defining moment for him. Ali Imron writes, "From there, my soul was moved to discourage the bad and enjoin the good and I became serious in my worship and study. I also had the wish to follow the struggle to defend Islam and the Muslim community from enemies like in Palestine and Afghanistan. Starting from that moment, I tried to do better than before."⁵ Inspired by that discussion, he wrote a letter to his elder brother, Muchlas—who was himself a veteran of the Soviet-Afghan War—expressing a desire to follow in his footsteps. Muchlas responded by saying Ali Imron could come to Malaysia after he graduated from high school, but he had to be ready to obey orders and follow leaders. That Muchlas expressed such ready confidence in his youngest brother was not surprising. The two were extremely close, and Muchlas had been teaching him about jihad, the Islamic state, and Darul Islam and its founder Kartosuwirjo from the time Ali Imron was just ten years old. For Ali Imron, at this point in his life, there was no doubt. A month after graduation, in August 1991, he flew to Malaysia with a group of guest workers.

My brother had gone to Afghanistan and Pakistan, so I felt I had the chance to follow. Actually, I only hoped to be like him. . . . When

> I arrived in Johor and met him again, I told him I wanted to go to
> school like he did in Afghanistan or Pakistan. I was ready to meet
> the requirements, to abandon everything. I was ready to listen and
> obey. I was ready. Muchlas said he would make a way.

Everything began to happen very fast. He was instructed to go to
Singapore for a visa. Then he was taken to see Abdullah Sungkar.
Before leaving for Pakistan, he was asked to take a loyalty oath,
swearing to obey the word of God and the Prophet. With the recit-
ing of the oath, he realized he had been inducted into the group.

Ali Imron's decision to join what was at the time an offshoot of
Darul Islam centered wholly on his brother. He was not recruited
into study circles. His entry into the group was not a gradual
process with various levels of caderization, as in the experience
of Anas. Unlike B.R., he was not galvanized by a specific conflict.
Since Muchlas was already a member in good standing, Ali Imron
had a shortcut to entry. From Ali Imron's perspective, he was not
seeking to join anything. He adored Muchlas and aspired to be
like him.

> I learned the lessons from Muchlas since I was a child. After I grew
> up and matured, I decided I wanted to join him. I was sure what-
> ever my brother did was right. It was the true path of Islam. At that
> moment, I didn't know much about the community. I was [only]
> informed in Afghanistan that the group was Darul Islam.

He arrived in Pakistan in the fall, on September 21, 1991, a mere
two months after graduating from high school. The Soviets had
withdrawn from Afghanistan two years earlier, but the camps still
continued to train fighters. He was met by other group members
in Peshawar, including Zulkarnaen, who would go on to become
JI's military commander. As Muchlas had instructed, he obeyed
their rules, changing his name and leaving his identity cards behind; Ali Imron was now Zaid.

The next day, he was escorted to the military academy run by Abdul Rasul Sayyaf, who led the training programs for Southeast Asians who had come to fight in the Soviet-Afghan War. He learned field engineering, tactics, map reading, and weapons training. He learned *fiqh jihad* (Islamic jurisprudence on jihad) so he could understand the Quran's rules of war and how to conduct himself in war. Nasir Abas, who would go on to head Mantiqi 3, JI's training region, was his instructor, and there were about thirty-five students in his class.

When he was in his third year at the camp, they were moved to Afghanistan, to Durkhom, near Jalalabad. He joined the war against the Afghan communists for just two months after graduation. But unlike Muchlas, who had fought in the Battle of the Lion's Den, he was unable to participate in actual battles.

> When I was there, the war was against the Afghan communists. On school holidays was the best time to go to the field of war. It was important to reach full skill. We were prepared to go to war. However, there was no war. All of us were crying. We thought there would be a war.

In 1995, the Taliban stated they would attack anyone who didn't join their effort in the civil war. With that directive, the Indonesians were instructed to pack their bags and return to Peshawar in preparation for going home. Ali Imron returned to Indonesia in 1996 and began teaching at the al Islam *pesantren* (Islamic boarding school) in Tenggulun, Lamongan, East Java, near his family home. He was reunited for a time with Ali Fauzi, his younger half brother, as both were instructed to help build the East Java branch of JI and to help with paramilitary training.

As early as 1996, Ali Imron began to gather bomb-making materials, weapons, and ammunition.

> I had tested bombs at the camp in Afghanistan. In Indonesia, it would be different. The first step is jihad preparation. Therefore,

I prepared the materials. I found bomb-making materials in chemical shops. We were sure that the preparation was crucial, just in case there would be a war or conflict. Although the jihad had not begun yet, the materials would be valuable, if there was a war.

Besides teaching at al Islam, I also participated in a meeting in 1998 facilitated by Ustad Zulkarnaen, who had since returned to Indonesia. I was to be part of a special team within Jemaah Islamiyah tasked with collecting ammunition, weapons, and other materials. This was only preparation. I had already begun doing this and had my own stock. In 1999, there was a mass killing of Muslims by Christians in Ambon on [the Muslim holy day of] Idul Fitri. What we imagined was coming true. The materials we had collected would be useful.

In the immediate aftermath of the Ambon riots, Zulkarnaen, the commander of the Laskar Khos, the paramilitary wing of JI, sent Ali Imron to Ambon to assess the situation and to manage activities on the ground. Together with Aris Munandar, Ali Imron laid the groundwork for what would become Mujahidin KOMPAK. Jemaah Islamiyah and KOMPAK would work very closely together during this period. JI fighters would travel to Ambon as part of Mujahidin KOMPAK, as JI was slow in responding to the Ambon conflict, and the two groups shared resources. In the summer of 1999, Ali Imron and others ran a three-month training session for new fighters at Waimorat on Buru island. When Ali Imron's duties were shifted to the Laskar Khos, he tasked his younger brother Ali Fauzi with taking over his role with Mujahidin KOMPAK. Ali Fauzi was quite happy to accept, having broken with JI by this time over the group's unwillingness to respond quickly enough to the Ambon conflict.

At this point, it is clear that Ali Imron was trusted within the inner circle of JI and within Zulkarnaen's special team, the Laskar

Khos. While he went back and forth to Ambon, his primary responsibilities were in teaching at al Islam *pesantren*. He also recruited his older brother Amrozi into the Laskar Khos, and it is a
testament to how much Zulkarnaen trusted Ali Imron that he accepted Amrozi, who had never been trained in either Afghanistan
or Mindanao.

It was during this same time between 2000 and 2002 that Hambali and Muchlas began to assemble a team, some of whom were
members of the Laskar Khos, to launch a series of bombings
aimed at Western and Christian targets, in the name of carrying
out Osama bin Laden's 1998 fatwa and hopefully setting off a civil
war between Muslims and Christians in Indonesia. Their attacks
included the Christmas Eve bombings in 2000, the bombing of
the Philippine ambassador's residence in 2000, the Atrium bombing in 2001, and the Bali bombing in 2002. Ali Imron played a
role in three of these bombings, preparing the bomb materials for
the Philippine ambassador's residence, setting off a bomb to blow
up a church in Mojokerto as part of the Christmas Eve bombing,
and then the Bali bombing. He contends that he found himself
questioning whether these actions were correct, but he deferred
to the wisdom of his seniors, who asserted that their actions were
justified.

In 2002, he met with Imam Samudra and Dulmatin in Solo.
Imam Samudra suggested setting off a bomb in Bali, but Ali Imron
rejected the suggestion, stating that it was better to assist the Muslims in Ambon and Poso. In August of that year, his elder brother
Amrozi asked him to reconsider Samudra's Bali proposal. When
they arrived at Dulmatin's house for another meeting, he found
that the plan for the Bali bombing was well under way and that
Muchlas had thrown his support behind it. Ali Imron again tried
to argue: "I asked whether this bombing was a true jihad. Muchlas

said that according to us, it was. I asked whether the brothers of JI had agreed to this sort of jihad. Muchlas replied, 'That is not your concern, it is my concern.'" Ali Imron repeatedly tried to appeal to his brother. "I was trying to warn him about whether our bombing plan was a real jihad or based on carnal desire."

When Ali Imron lost the argument, however, he consented to go along, initially being tasked only with helping Amrozi procure and prepare the car in Lamongan. Originally, Imam Samudra planned for the bombing to mark the anniversary of September 11, 2001, but the others protested that there was not enough time to ready the materials and carry out the operation. They settled on the date of October 12. Muchlas became the team leader. Ali Imron surveyed the tourist areas, at Imam Samudra's request, to determine which clubs had the largest number of foreigners. They began to make preparations. Ali Imron again voiced his opposition to this attack.

> When the bomb arrived in Bali on September 25, I told Muchlas via Amrozi that I thought when the bomb exploded, things would get messy. [People were starting] to acknowledge Indonesia as a hub of terrorism. Abu Bakar Ba'asyir had been accused of involvement in Malaysia and Singapore. There was also news about Ngruki. If the bomb in Bali exploded, it would validate those accusations. I asked whether the bombing was a JI program and agreed upon by all. Muchlas said it was so. Personally, I disagreed. However, I was a junior member and also a younger brother. . . . At the time, I did not win the argument with them, so I had to follow them. My hope was at the time that the bombing would have a positive impact on our fight. I followed because I trusted my seniors in JI.

He notes, "We did not discuss whether the bombing was allowed. The action was based on the decree of Osama bin Laden, stating that it was allowed to bomb such a place. The most important part was targeting as many foreigners as possible."

Ali Imron was conflicted. On the one hand, he opposed the targeting of civilians in such attacks unless those civilians were brutalizing Muslims, as was the case in Ambon and Poso. On the other hand, when he lost the argument, he felt bound by loyalty to his brothers and his group to follow along and do his part. Moreover, he was happy when the bombing was successful. He explains,

> As a person opposed to the Bali bombing action, I was in doubt. I was happy after the program was on target, that the bomb exploded. Yet I doubted that such a bombing was true jihad. Would this action have a positive impact on the jihads in Ambon and other places? These were my feelings on the night when the bomb exploded.

Thus, Ali Imron's initial concerns were based on rational assessment. What would the consequences of these actions be? Prior to this point, JI members had been able to move around quite freely. Few had hit the Indonesian government's radar, despite iterated attacks like the Christmas Eve bombings and the Atrium bombing. Would this action have blowback effects for JI as an organization? Would it have negative consequences for what he viewed as the legitimate jihads in Ambon and Poso? And what of the Quran's rules of war? He knew it was forbidden to kill civilians indiscriminately, yet this attack would do just that. He knew that before a legitimate jihad action is undertaken, the enemies must first be warned. Did these people view Muslims as their enemies? They were just tourists. However, in the end, Ali Imron went along with the plan and felt happy about it afterward. Thus, whatever resistant thoughts occurred, they were not strong enough to counterbalance the pull of loyalty he felt to his brothers and to the group of friends who were involved in this operation.

Two weeks after the bombing, the team met together for an evaluation. After having some time to reflect, Ali Imron spoke his mind and expressed his disappointment in the action.

> I protested that the preparation of the bombing was terrible and not well planned. We would be easily arrested, as Amrozi borrowed the car from someone who knew him very well. The suicide bomber could not drive. I myself had to drive the car. What do we do now? What is the message and image of our movement? What was our jihad with such a bombing? If we had a jihad against the government, why not attack the police or the TNI [Tentara Nasional Indonesia, the Indonesian National Army]? Muchlas said that was outside our plan. I was angry. I said if the jihad was to develop an Islamic state, let's fight against the Indonesian government. Muchlas again said that it was not yet planned.

When Amrozi was arrested on January 5, 2003, Ali Imron's disillusionment deepened further.

> I warned them. When Amrozi was caught after the Bali bombing, this was a sign that our jihad was wrong. Why? Because jihad needs to generate something positive, just like what the Prophet did. From the start to the end, because the jihad was right, the Prophet won and got positive results. But with the arrest of Amrozi, it meant the jihad was wrong. I became more aware that this kind of fighting has to stop. After Imam Samudra was arrested, I became more and more aware. That really showed me that what we did was a mistake in jihad.

Ali Imron watched as the police arrested Amrozi, then Imam Samudra, then Muchlas, and became increasingly convinced that God was not on their side in this operation. Yet he chose to run rather than surrender because he knew that, if he were arrested, as deeply involved in the attack as he had been, the outcome would not be good for him. Moreover, he feared the judgment of his friends. If he surrendered, would he be labeled a traitor? Eight days after the arrest of Amrozi, the police found and arrested Ali Imron in Kalimantan, together with his friend, Mubarok, who had played a very minor role in the Bali bombing. Ali Imron chose not to fight. Instead, he cooperated with the authorities—answering their questions. He admitted his own fault. After processing, he was sent to Kerobokan prison and put in a special section with Amrozi, Muchlas, and Imam Samudra. He decided to cooperate attitudinally as well. "When I was arrested, I decided to behave differently than [Muchlas and Amrozi]. I had to respect the Balinese, who were Hindu. That is what differentiated them and me. I was polite during the trial." He refused to share their lawyer from the Muslim Defenders Team, seeking out his own attorney to represent his interests. When Ali Imron was about to request a pardon from the president to take the death penalty off the table, Muchlas appealed to him to stop, but he refused, asserting his independence. "I would not be managed by Muchlas anymore." He was also publicly remorseful.

> I was visited by the victim witnesses, those who lost their family members, their breadwinners. Some were Muslims. I was sad. . . . I asked mercy from God and sought forgiveness from the victims, families and parties that had lost so much because of me.

As a result of his cooperation and remorseful attitude, he received a twenty-year sentence, in contrast to his elder siblings and Samudra, who were sentenced to death.

After deciding to cooperate, he pushed to be reassigned from the special lockup with Imam Samudra, Muchlas, and Amrozi, contending that since he had adopted a more constructive attitude compared to his brothers and Samudra, he should not receive the same treatment. He was subsequently reassigned to the J block, which held people not directly involved in the Bali bombing. This was an interesting decision on Ali Imron's part. In physically breaking away from his older brothers, he effectively removed himself from their orbit. In doing so, he became increasingly comfortable with his own position regarding his role in the Bali bombing and his view about the use of bombings of civilian targets more generally as a tactic.

In Ali Imron's narrative to this point, several aspects are apparent. While in Muchlas's orbit, Ali Imron felt disillusioned by bombings against civilian targets. He saw this side project by Muchlas and Hambali as something that, in all likelihood, would not end well. He spoke up and attempted to dissuade Muchlas and the others from undertaking the Bali bombing, but when they decided to mount the attack anyway, he went along, seeing himself as a junior member and a younger brother, bound by the duty to obey his seniors.

In the aftermath of the Bali bombing, when the costs of the attack became apparent, when Muchlas and Amrozi were arrested, Ali Imron grew more confident in his convictions. Together with Mubarok, his friend who played a small role in the Bali bombing, he began assessing the costs of using bombings in peaceful areas, costs counted in terms of civilian deaths. The combination of disillusionment and cost-benefit analysis was further reinforced by his disappointment with himself—the key role he played in the Bali bombing and his disappointment with JI leaders who masterminded these bombings. "I am disappointed because they [Hambali and Muchlas] made plans and executed them without discussing it with the other members. As senior leaders, they should have been able to think of a better way." He also expressed his wish that Abu Bakar Ba'asyir had been firmer in his statements to the bombers and about bombings more generally. "If he took some steps to prevent such actions, the members would think, 'Oh look, Ustad Abu disagreed with the idea; we don't have to do it.' This made me disappointed." Had Hambali and Muchlas consulted with JI's Markaziyah, their central command, plans for the Bali bombing might have been headed off. If Ustad Abu Bakar Ba'asyir had spoken out more forcefully, perhaps Ali Imron might have "won the argument."

Yet Ali Imron does not speak harshly about Muchlas. His accepts that his brother had this influence on him and that the trajectory of his brother's life shaped his.

> I became like this because of Muchlas. I went to Afghanistan because of Muchlas. I know how to fight because of Muchlas. I am jailed because of Muchlas. But when there is a mistake, we need to admit it. I should not follow what they [Muchlas and Amrozi] did when they were arrested and say that I did not regret what I did. We need to admit when we do wrong things so it can be a lesson for others.

In a perhaps unintentionally symbolic gesture, Ali Imron physically broke from his brothers, demanding reassignment to a different block in Kerobokan prison. While he would not castigate his brother, he would no longer live in his shadow. Not long after that, he and Mubarok, who was also cooperating, were moved to POLDA Metrojaya in Jakarta to serve out the remainder of their sentences.

In 2006, Ali Imron achieved a small victory for himself personally. His younger half brother, Ali Fauzi, had returned from the Philippines, where he had fled in the aftermath of the Bali bombing, fearing being caught up in the police dragnet. Ali Imron was deeply concerned that his brother might fall in with bombing masterminds Noordin M. Top and Dr. Azhari, given his close friendship with the latter. When the brothers were reunited at POLDA Metro, after some brief police questioning, they shared their views on the Bali bombing and the permissibility of bombing attacks. Ali Imron was able to convince Ali Fauzi of the rightness of his perspective.

During Ali Imron's time in prison, he has come to have confidence in his own views on the right and wrong kind of jihad. His revised perspective, independent of the influence of his late elder brothers, centers on the right time, targets, locations, and conditions. Interestingly, he contends he held these views all along. However, now he has the strength of mind to go his own way.

> Bombings like the Philippine ambassador's residence, the churches during Christmas nights, the Atrium Mall, and Bali need to be stopped. These things are not appropriate. If we return to knowledge of jihad or *fiqh jihad*, they are called offensive jihad, attacking a certain party that we think of as the enemy in the first place. However, offensive jihad needs some phases and can't be done right now since we do not have administrative zones. Since the very beginning, I said that if we conducted offensive jihad without power, it would result in danger or it would disadvantage our fight. Jihad as a purpose is not wrong. The wrong thing is the method. My involvement in Ambon was not a mistake. In Ambon, it was right, and until the end of time, it will always be right. My jihad by going to Afghanistan was correct. . . . The mistake was the [use of] bombings. Until the day I die, I will do jihad and will always have a passion to do it. I will not do jihad [in a manner divergent from that] of our ancestors. I will not bomb a place without reason. If I cannot do jihad in Indonesia, I will just leave. When I am in Indonesia, I will do *dakwah* whether it is about jihad or about Islam.

I will do this without being against the current situation [one where Indonesia is not an Islamic state].

Ali Imron's view has shaped many who have subsequently disengaged from JI either by leaving the movement or by migrating from a violent to nonviolent role within the movement. He makes several important points that echo in the general JI discourse. First, there is a difference between bombings and jihad in a conflict zone, and the former is inappropriate and counterproductive to JI's goals as a movement. Second, he stresses the importance of timing, targets, locations, and conditions: the Bali bombing and Christmas Eve bombings, among others, were wrong because the timing of the attacks, and the targets chosen for those attacks, were wrong. Third, he stresses that at this time, Indonesia is not an appropriate place to conduct jihad because it is peaceful and safe. In interviews, this author has heard those points stated again and again. This is not surprising. As part of his plea deal, Ali Imron agreed to lead formal and informal discussions with individual jihadists and small group discussions. Thus, his view has become socialized within many circles of JI.

If he were let out of prison, he says, he would focus on preaching, using his life and the mistakes he made as lessons for others.

[I would prioritize] preaching to my fellow friends so they will not conduct wrong jihads because it is against the Sunnah and the spirit of jihad itself. I will ask them not to do jihads that are not in line with the tactics and strategies in Islam. That is the most important thing to me, and on every occasion, I say that. At least that can be a lesson for them and make them think before doing things. I am trying to be released so I can preach freely. Whatever I do here, because I am jailed, my friends say, "Ali Imron is like that because he is jailed and pressured by the government and police."

In working toward this goal, he would have a partner in Ali Fauzi. In Lamongan, there would be a mutual aid society to welcome him home and help him reintegrate into society. Should communal violence break out in Ambon or Poso, however, he would have few qualms taking up arms again in a legitimate jihad.

Ali Imron's disengagement narrative is less complex than that of Anas or B.R. or Ali Fauzi. That he is in prison limits his ability to develop new friendships. Instead, his disengagement is driven by a combination of two factors that reinforce each other: a rational assessment that bombings are not permitted according to Islam and have negative consequences for the movement and the goals it seeks to achieve; and a broad disillusionment with the tactics and leaders who planned such bombings, as well as disillusionment with his own role. It is these factors that led Ali Imron to gain confidence and strength in the views he held prior to his participation in terror attacks, to separate himself from his elder siblings, and to teach that perspective to others.

Ali Imron still considers himself to be a member of JI. In prison now, he is physically disengaged from the movement; and even if he were not in prison, he would be viewed as having migrated from a violent to a nonviolent role within JI. He does not know how he is viewed by JI members on the outside, however. "I never withdrew from JI. It is possible I've been expelled. I will never pull my loyalty oath to [the late] Ustad Abdullah Sungkar." Ali Imron goes on to explain that while he remains loyal to JI, that does not mean he will blindly follow others. "I don't want to be managed by the others. I make my own decisions. No one has the right to control me."

6

Ali Fauzi

According to the Prophet, the more friends you have, the more feedback you get. I used to mingle with JI members. My circle of friends was limited. But it has changed now.

—*Ali Fauzi*

Ali Fauzi is the younger half brother of Muchlas, Amrozi, and Ali Imron. Separated in age by less than a year, Ali Fauzi and Ali Imron largely grew up together, though they lived in separate houses. The two of them attended the same Muhammadiyah elementary and middle schools. When Ali Imron was sent to Ngruki, the hard-line Islamic boarding school, Ali Fauzi was sent along too. But they both soon returned home, one after the other. Following Ali Fauzi's return home from Ngruki, his parents sent him to high school at another *pesantren*, this one a Salafi school in the nearby district of Kertosono, which offered a general curriculum in the morning and religious classes in the afternoon. After three years, he followed his friends to Ma'had Ali, the next level of *pesantren* education after secondary school; but finding the curriculum too similar to what he had already been learning, he dropped out.

Around this time, an envelope came in the mail addressed to him and postmarked Afghanistan. Inside were two letters, one for him and one for Ali Imron. In his letter, his elder half brother Muchlas exhorted them to join him. Ali Fauzi describes the contents of the letter. "Muchlas asked me to be a true *mu'mim*, a true Muslim. A *mu'mim* who understands jihad. . . . I was happy [to receive the letter] because at the time, war was raging between the Afghans and the Soviets. The letter was written in Arabic. I felt like I was receiving a calling." Not long after he left boarding school, some two months after Ali Imron's departure for Pakistan, Ali Fauzi left for Malaysia. He was eighteen.

When Ali Fauzi met Muchlas after his arrival in Kuala Lumpur, Malaysia, they had not seen each other in seven or eight years. As a test, Muchlas asked him who Kartosuwirjo was. Ali Imron, groomed by Muchlas since the age of ten, would have answered, "An Islamic fighter." However, Ali Fauzi responded, "I know him. He was a rebel." Muchlas retorted that Kartosuwirjo was the icon of his struggle.

Viewing Ali Fauzi as clearly not ideologically or mentally ready to follow Ali Imron to Afghanistan, Muchlas invited Ali Fauzi to help him build an Islamic boarding school in Malaysia's Johor State, what would become Luqmanul Hakim. Perhaps indicative of the distance between these two brothers, Ali Fauzi was not immediately welcomed into the group as Ali Imron had been. First, he would have to prove himself. However, his work with Muchlas in building the school would be a bonding experience, and through that experience he would be socialized into the group and come to share their thinking, particularly about jihad.

> I built the *pesantren* with my own hands. Muchlas and I. From 1991, I began to know who Muchlas really was and what his group was about. I was introduced to them. I followed their daily routines. I joined in their *taklim* [religious study groups]. Automatically, my frame of thinking became influenced by them. When they

thought I was qualified enough to be a member of the organization, I was given the oath of loyalty. [I swore] to Abdullah Sungkar
that I would be obedient and loyal. After I had taken the oath, I
automatically became a part of the *ikhwan* of NII/DI. When the
split occurred in 1993, I was given the oath again.

He remarked that at the second *bai'at* (loyalty oath), there were
hundreds of other members. Those who refused to swear the oath
to JI were sent home. With that second communal oath experience, his commitment to the group became stronger.

The radicalization process with Ali Fauzi is clear. He was brought
into JI via Muchlas, his older, much respected half brother. He was
gradually brought into the group and socialized into their activities after proving himself by helping to build Luqmanul Hakim
and teaching there. When he was finally deemed ready, he was
given the loyalty oath, promising to hear and obey. Once this occurred, the next step of his radicalization commenced. They began
to groom him for jihad.

Ali Fauzi contends he knew little about jihad prior to his socialization into the group. "When I was in *pesantren* in Indonesia, I understood nothing [about jihad]. It was only at Luqmanul
Hakim that I was introduced to war videos—Afghanistan, Bosnia.
From that, I became interested in becoming like them." The study
of *fiqh jihad* and the war videos shaped Ali Fauzi's thinking. He
began to long to go fight in a jihad, die as a *syahid* (martyr) and go
to heaven. After three years, Muchlas finally assessed him as ready
for jihad.

I was ready to go. At that point, he asked, "Do you want to go to
Afghanistan or Moro?" I replied, "Which place still has war?" He
responded, "Moro. The war goes on every day with the Philippine
government." So I chose to go there.

Muchlas subsequently connected Ali Fauzi to Hambali, who was then responsible for Sabah and Mindanao. Ali Fauzi left Johor for Sabah, using a fake passport, made his way to Sandakan, and was smuggled on a ship repatriating Filipino workers from Malaysia. He entered Camp Abu Bakar and joined the Mujahidin Military Academy. Over the next three years, he trained in weapons, tactics, infantry, and field engineering. He participated in jihad for only a short time, after which he was assigned to man an MILF guard post. He contends that this was a happy time for him, echoing the same themes as Anas, Agus, and Ali Imron about the joys of jihad. In 1997, however, he was instructed to go back to Malaysia, where he was offered the opportunity to teach yet again at Luqmanul Hakim; but he refused, preferring to go to Kuala Lumpur and become just an ordinary JI member participating in everyday activities. Ali Imron, by this time, was already in East Java, gathering weapons and bomb-making materials. In 1998, following the May riots, the brothers were given a common duty, to help build the JI branch in East Java, and were finally reunited.

Ali Fauzi would stay in East Java for two years, tasked to provide paramilitary training. When the Ambon conflict broke out, Ali Imron, on Zulkarnaen's orders, left for Ambon to provide assistance. In light of the outbreak of a legitimate jihad front in Indonesia, Ali Fauzi became insistent that participants receive full paramilitary training, to be taught to use weapons and make bombs. He began to wonder why JI was not sending volunteers. JI convened a big meeting in June of 1999 to assess whether or not to send troops to Ambon. When his seniors determined that it was too premature to send fighters, Ali Fauzi disagreed. He pushed them. "I wanted a big JI presence in Ambon. My opinion was not accepted. Therefore I quit."

For Ali Fauzi, JI's reluctance to commit troops to Ambon was inexcusable. Indonesian Muslims were under threat. He felt compelled to go.

> This is *jihad difaa'i*, a defensive jihad. A defensive jihad is serious. If we have the ability, we must defend [the Muslims]. This is an individual obligation. At the time, as someone with the capability to make weapons, to make bombs, to kill, I felt the calling. How could I not go there? I would be sinning otherwise.

Thus, Ali Fauzi shifted his allegiance and joined Mujahidin KOMPAK, which was far quicker to commit troops.

> It was precisely because JI was too slow that I left. I was then taken in by my friend, Aris Munandar, to foster KOMPAK. It was a match made in heaven. I was grateful for the opportunity. He was pleased that I joined him. He told me to organize friends in Ambon. I went there, and with [others] we ran short paramilitary trainings on Buru Island and areas around Ambon. The conflict continued. I moved back and forth from Ambon to Java, bringing explosives and weapons. This went on for more than a year.

During this time in Ambon, Ali Fauzi was reunited with his brothers Ali Imron and Amrozi. There, in Ambon, they taught Amrozi, who had not attended any military academy, to use weapons and make bombs. They took him on a camping trip and taught him to shoot.

Following the Walisongo massacre in May 2001, Ali Fauzi was sent to Poso and began organizing the youth who had remained behind after everyone else had fled. He explains:

> They were drunk. We raised their awareness, and they wanted to join us because we had brought weapons to the area. . . . We took them to the mountains and trained them in how to assemble

bombs, how to shoot, and in [paramilitary] tactics. They became more confident. After we finished training them, we sent them back to their villages.

He stayed in Poso for five months, after which he returned home to Lamongan and resumed teaching at *pesantren* al Islam, traveling periodically to Ambon and Poso.

When the Bali bombing occurred, on October 12, 2002, Ali Fauzi assessed the situation and decided it was no longer safe. Hearing a rumor about a National Police blacklist, which allegedly included not only suspects in the bombing but known fighters in Ambon and Poso, he left his home and slowly began to make his way back to the Philippines. When his brothers were arrested, he was already on the run. When the news of his brothers' arrest reached him, he was safely in Sabah, Malaysia. "I cried when I heard the news. I cried because they are my brothers." He crossed into the Philippines and made his way back to MILF territory, where he would stay until 2006. He became a trainer again.

In examining Ali Fauzi's behavior to this point, it is clear that, even though he was indoctrinated by Muchlas and was part of the group around Luqmanul Hakim, men who would mastermind some of Indonesia's worst bombings, Ali Fauzi retained an independent streak in his thinking. In contrast with Ali Imron, who followed his brother Muchlas even when he knew in his heart that the bombing action was not right, Ali Fauzi did not seem as committed to "I hear and I obey," when doing so ran contrary to his own sense of right and wrong. He would defer to Muchlas in discussions, for example, of Osama bin Laden's fatwa, based on a sense of obeying one's seniors. When he had to decide whether or not to take action, however, he asserted independence. For Ali Fauzi, jihad actions were to be confined to legitimate conflict zones, and when there was an opportunity to participate in a jihad action in a war zone, one must do it.

Ali Fauzi would disengage from violence and reintegrate into society perhaps more successfully than anyone else in this book, but it would take years. First, he needed to process the Bali bombing itself, and that took time and observation. His first real opportunity to do this was when Umar Patek, one of the participants in the bombing, arrived in the Philippines. "Umar Patek and I always discussed about the Bali bombing and whether it was the right thing to do or not. I had been close to Umar Patek since we were together at Hudaibiyah [JI's training camp in the Philippines]. Umar said that he disagreed with the bombing, but he was assigned by Muchlas to the team. So like it or not, he became a subordinate." For the next four years, Ali Fauzi kept company with Bali bombing fugitives Dulmatin, Umar Patek, and others who were hiding out. From the Philippines, he watched as JI was revealed to the nation and as JI members' participation in other bombings became known. When the leadership of the MILF changed in 2006, he and the other Indonesians were asked to leave the Philippines.

After Ali Fauzi returned home to Indonesia, Ali Imron reached out to his brother via a student with a message that Ali Fauzi should come to Jakarta to visit him in jail. When they spoke over the phone, Ali Imron pushed: "'Just come over here. There were no police dossiers that mentioned your involvement; you were only mentioned for your activities in Ambon and Poso.'" The brothers were very happy to see each other again, after having been separated for so long. They sat down together in the small cell at POLDA Metro that had been Ali Imron's home for the past four years. Ali Imron was deeply concerned for Ali Fauzi, for he knew his brother had been very close with the master bomber Dr. Azhari during his time at Luqmanul Hakim. According to Ali Fauzi, "He feared that if he did not get me to his side, Dr. Azhari and Noordin M. Top would recruit me." Therefore, Ali Imron sought to set his brother on the correct path. In an interview I had with both men in 2014, Ali Imron explains how he *knew* he could do it:

> I know who my brother is. Ali Fauzi differed from Amrozi, Muchlas, and me in his thoughts on jihad. He helped our jihad endeavor in Ambon and Poso, which were sites of conflict. But when I asked him to assist us in detonating bombs, he refused to do it. Then I knew the difference between me and him. Hence, when I had different arguments with Muchlas, Amrozi, and Imam Samudra when we were arrested, I believed that Ali Fauzi would share my opinion.

Ali Fauzi then added, "I had an emotional tie to him as well. When he missed classes in Islamic boarding school, I was always his replacement. When I missed classes, he was my replacement." Ali Fauzi did not say whether Ali Imron's concerns were warranted. However, he admits that he did not fully arrive at the conclusion that the Bali bombing was wrong until after he sat down with Ali Imron. They shared their views on the Bali bombing, about how bombings in non-conflict areas would yield more losses than benefits. It had cost the jihadi community so much. It had cast a stain on the Muslim community. By the end of the conversation, Ali Fauzi was convinced. It must have been a tremendous relief for Ali Imron when he knew Ali Fauzi was on his side. He then began to push Ali Fauzi to stay in Indonesia, to keep to the straight path, and to return to school for a university degree.

Around this same time, Ali Fauzi's son revealed to him that a man named Noor Huda Ismail had been visiting their home, while he had been away in the Philippines. He had checked in on the children and brought them presents. Who was this Noor Huda Ismail who was visiting his children? He had been a classmate of Ali

Fauzi's half brother Jabir, who had died climbing Mount Lawu; he was a friend of the family. He would visit Ali Imron as well, and sometimes their visits would coincide. In 2009, Noor Huda would start a terrorist rehabilitation NGO, the Institute for International Peace Building. At that time, however, he was in the process of figuring out how to help men like Ali Fauzi. Noor Huda also began pressuring him to go to college.

Disengagement was so slow for Ali Fauzi because of the time it took him to process the costs and benefits of bombing actions. In the abstract, Ali Fauzi had long been confident in the view that violence was legitimate only in conflict areas. When faced with a bombing that involved three of his half brothers, however, he was at a loss. Processing this loss from exile in the Philippines proved inadequate. It took coming home and discussing the matter with Ali Imron to fully comprehend what had happened and how he felt about it. It was wise of Ali Imron to seek out his brother and to convince him of the correctness of the anti-bombing view. Shortly after the execution of Muchlas, Amrozi, and Imam Samudra in 2008, many began coming to Ali Fauzi asking for training in how to build bombs and claiming that Muchlas and Amrozi's testaments had ordered them to do it. Ali Fauzi contends that he did not believe them and refused to give them training. "Bomb-making knowledge is very dangerous if misused. I would not transfer my dangerous knowledge, because it is dangerous to Indonesia as a country. If I taught someone how to build bombs, I'd be responsible for his actions."

He did not want to go backward, only forward. With pressure and support from Ali Imron and Noor Huda Ismail, he began considering the next steps. In 2009, he returned to school. In considering where to attend university, he decided to return to his familial roots in Muhammadiyah and enrolled in Muhammadiyah

University–Surabaya to study Islamic education. That same year, he began lecturing at Sekolah Tinggi Agama Islam Muhammadiyah (STAIM) and Sekolah Tinggi Ilmu Tarbiyah (STIT), two schools of tertiary education in Islamic studies that exist in an educational middle ground between high school and university. He contends that he decided to go back to school

> to open up a new chapter in my life. I began to become more deliberative when I studied in university. . . . I cultivated my knowledge through going to university. . . . When I taught at Luqmanul Hakim, it only went up through junior high school. The lessons were flat. We emphasized *tauhid* [monotheism]. At Muhammadiyah University, I learned more advanced subjects. I learned about public affairs. About the split in Islam. About different groups in Islam, the *khawarij, jurji'ah, sayai'ah, mutazilah.*

He was learning about Islam in a very sophisticated way, an intellectual way that he found more challenging than what he had taught at Luqmanul Hakim or learned during his studies at the boarding school at Kertosono or at Ma'had Ali. This gave him tools to rethink his views in a manner based in Islamic law and thought. Moreover, he began to make new friends, and this exposed him to a wider range of viewpoints.

> I made new friends. They contributed to changing my mind. According to the Prophet Muhammad, the more friends you have, the more feedback you get. I used to mingle with JI members. My circle of friends was limited. But it has changed now. Now, I get to know you as well.

Over the course of his studies, Ali Fauzi also experienced an ideological return to his roots. He had been born into a Muhammadiyah family. He went to Muhammadiyah elementary and middle schools. Therefore it was not surprising that in leaving JI and Mujahidin KOMPAK, he returned to Muhammadiyah. His ability to reintegrate into society via Muhammadiyah was tremendously helpful and empowering to him. He felt welcomed back to Muhammadiyah; there was no stigma directed toward him for his prior activities. "Muhammadiyah took me in as a student. I was applauded by Muhammadiyah lecturers and invited by Muhammadiyah University–Malang to meet with an American postgraduate lecturer named Maria." It is perhaps with Ali Fauzi that we see evidence of ideological deradicalization, in part because of his background as a teacher and in part because of the rigorous course of Islamic study he embarked on as part of his reintegration.

In 2011, Ali Fauzi was offered an opportunity that solidified many of the conclusions he had been coming to independently and enabled him to understand and cultivate empathy toward the victims of terror attacks. He participated in a workshop in Ireland called Broaden Ideas, which brought terrorists and victims of terrorism together and included terrorists from Jewish, Muslim, and Hindu extremist groups, as well as former Irish Republican Army members. "I met Feby and Max Boon, whose leg was amputated. I felt sad. I felt pity for innocent people who did not know about jihad affairs and became victims of bombings. I was very sad. I was thinking about what if it had occurred in my own family."

Ali Fauzi also began to connect with other veterans of the Soviet-Afghan War, the Mindanao conflict, the Ambon and the Poso conflicts, and together they started a mutual aid society in the town of Lamongan, which included a goat-breeding cooperative and a discussion group to analyze, challenge, and work through some of their previously held views (see chapter 8 for further details). After ISIS became popular in Lamongan, they extended the discussion group to include families of imprisoned terrorists.

There are several interesting points to note. First, Ali Fauzi's re-integration was successful in large part because he found a second ideological and spiritual home in Muhammadiyah, a movement he was born into and that he felt mirrored his own personal religious outlook to a significant degree. Second, in being embraced by Muhammadiyah, rather than stigmatized and alienated, he was able to make new friends and learn of different viewpoints. Third, that he had the full support of Ali Imron was certainly empowering to him. He was living on the outside for both of them, succeeding for both of them. Finally, in disengaging and reintegrating, he did not fully sever ties with the other jihadists. He no longer views himself as a member of Mujahidin KOMPAK, and he had long since broken with JI. Just because he turned away and made new friends, however, did not mean he abandoned old ones. He refused to share "dangerous" knowledge that he had accumulated in his years fighting in jihad and working as a trainer. He could not trust that those he trained would not use the knowledge in Indonesia. However, he would certainly help those in need, providing scholarships for children to study at al Islam *pesantren*, and, through his mutual aid society, providing a network of solidarity for those going through the processes of disengagement and reintegration.

7

Yuda

My only regret is that I did not kill more people. That
is all.

—*Yuda*

Of the five life histories examined in detail in this book, "Yuda"
was chosen as an example of someone who remained committed to the cause of violence. Thus, Yuda presents an important
counterpoint to B.R., Anas, Ali Imron, and Ali Fauzi, not only for
his perspective but also for the factors that influenced him to retain such a radical position.

Yuda was born in the Gebangrejo neighborhood of Poso. He left
school following junior high school. He was educated in public
schools, in contrast to B.R., who attended Islamic school with al
Chairat. Prior to the outbreak of the communal conflict, Yuda was
a drug dealer, a livestock rustler, and a rock musician of some re-
nown on the island of Sulawesi, playing gigs from Gorontalo in the
north of the island all the way to Makassar in the south. Prior to
the conflict, he had had many Christian friends. When the conflict
initially broke out as tit-for-tat bouts of gang violence in December 1998, Yuda paid it little mind, continuing to perform with his
band, drink, and do drugs.

However, the Walisongo massacre on May 28, 2000, marked a decisive shift in Yuda's attitude and thinking. As seen from B.R.'s recollection, Walisongo radicalized a number of Poso jihadis, but for Yuda, it was intensely personal, as his extended family was among the victims.

> Twenty-two of my relatives were slain. I personally collected the bodies. I was appointed by the subdistrict office to the evaluation team in Kilometer 9 [site of the massacre]. I discovered the bodies of my aunt and cousins. My aunt was naked except for her jilbab. They raped her. They were so cruel. My relatives were dead. That is when I stopped drinking, doing drugs, and playing music. At the time, I was not religious. I had not begun attending *majelis taklim* [gatherings for the study of the Quran]. At the time, I just wanted to obtain a weapon. My in-laws had some property; I sold it for twelve million rupiah and spent it on an Uzi. I had no idea about jihad then. I just wanted to kill.

The brutal rape and murder of his aunt and murder of his cousins evoked in Yuda a desire for revenge. He bought a gun. Then he began to kill. "I started killing. Sometimes, I did it alone. Sometimes with others." Revenge killing had become his priority.

In the weeks following the Walisongo massacre, JI members, "*ustads* from Java," began arriving and setting up *taklim* in the local mosques. Yuda's friends had begun attending the *taklim*. He was invited to join them later that year, and out of curiosity he began to go along. There, in the *taklim*, he learned about Islam, "the meaning of jihad," "how to wage jihad," and "how to recognize a *kafir*." He learned that Christians in Poso were infidels who needed to be killed, as opposed to "people of the book," with whom coexistence was possible. The lessons he learned in the *taklim* legitimated the desire for revenge he already felt and led him to adopt a new worldview and set of social relations.

> Before I joined the fight, I played in Lembomawo, a Christian area. Many of my friends were Christians. I rarely came to Poso. However, [after Walisongo], I cut off my relations with the Christians. Because Christians killed Muslims in Poso. And because after I understood what jihad meant, I knew who the infidels were.

Increasingly, his social circle was confined to his friends in Tanah Runtuh and affiliated groups. His younger brothers joined as well. He had effectively traded his gang of bandmates for a jihad gang. In 2001, he was invited to participate in paramilitary training, in which he improved his skills with machine guns and learned to make proper bombs.

In December 2001, the Malino peace accords were signed. Yuda expressed his disdain for the agreement, using the language of revenge. "The Malino agreement was detrimental to the interests of the Poso Muslims because it came about after [the Christian militias] massacred our people. How could Muslims retaliate if they were bound by such an agreement?"

By 2002, Hasanuddin, a Javanese member of JI who had trained at Camp Hudaibiyah, JI's military academy in the Philippines, arrived in Tanah Runtuh as the new leader of JI-Poso. He gathered together the members of Tanah Runtuh, organizing them into a *dakwah* wing and a two-tiered paramilitary wing. Yuda was part of the paramilitary wing, some of whom would be responsible for planning and executing major attacks against mostly Christian targets between 2003 and 2006.[1] According to Yuda, the selection process went as follows: "We'd meet for a briefing. Everyone proposed their targets, and then we discussed them. Hasanuddin would then give his approval."

Between 2004 and 2006, Yuda participated in numerous terrorist attacks and actions in support of those attacks, including the robbery of a gold shop in the Palu market in January 2004; the assault on the Maranatha market in Donggala on January 24, 2004; the killing of the priest Susianti Tinulele on July 18, 2004, at the Effata church in Palu; the mutilation of the village head, Pinedapa Sarminales Ndele, on November 3, 2004; the bombing of the Anugrah church on December 12, 2004; the mutilation of the schoolgirls on October 29, 2005, in Poso; the shooting of Ivone Natalia Moganti on November 8, 2005; the bombing of the Eklesia church on July 1, 2006; and the bombing of the door of GOR Pusalemba in Poso on August 3, 2006.[2] Yuda noted that of all of these, "the most satisfying action was the killing of the priest. That was really satisfying. Because he was an infidel. I was the executioner. Everyone knew it was me. That it was my task."

On January 22, 2007, Densus 88 raided the Tanah Runtuh compound. Yuda was caught shortly thereafter. He details the story of his capture.

> I was assigned to Jalan Pulau Seram. We were beaten back near the governor's office. . . . I got shot and fell. My friends hid me in a chicken shack and took me to Suster Nuha, where I slept. There were police everywhere. At dawn, I left and headed to Gunung Harjati, the governor's office, which has a through pass to Kayamanya. I left on foot. I fell every thirty meters. I was losing blood. Once I reached Kayamanya, I was evacuated to Landangan and [then] Lawanga. I met up with [my friend]. All roads into and out of Poso had been closed, so we stuck together. We saw cops on the street on motorcycle. I really wanted to shoot them, to take them out one at a time. [My friend] thought we should avoid them and find a friend and a safe place to stay. We headed for a friend's house. We hadn't even settled into sleep for fifteen minutes when we were surrounded. They shouted for us to get out. We kept quiet. I told

[my friend] we should fight back; I didn't want to die in the house. It was better to die with dignity than live with shame. [My friend] agreed, but we only had one pistol between us. [My friend] let me go first and shot to cover me. I ran to the sea and found a boat. I spent the night with my aunt. Then they caught me.

Yuda contends he was tortured mercilessly following his arrest. "They stripped me naked. They used wires. They rolled up a newspaper and stabbed me in the face with it till I bled. They beat me with full water bottles. They shoved one up my backside. It was really painful. They kept asking me, 'Where are the weapons?' I answered they had all been seized." As a result of the torture he experienced, the target of his revenge has widened from Christian "infidels" to the police as well. "I never regret what I did. I swear to Allah. I don't regret being here [in prison]. I wish I had killed more infidel police officers before I went to jail."

Yuda claimed his parents supported his actions. His two brothers were killed in the Densus 88 raid on Tanah Runtuh on January 22, 2007; one was shot and the other was taken alive and died during the interrogation. When Densus 88 could not find Yuda, they went to his parents. The authorities invited him to surrender, contending if he did, none of his friends would be tortured. However, his parents impressed on him the importance of rejecting the offer, fearing for his safety at the hands of the police. "They said if I surrendered, they would kill me." His father refused to betray his whereabouts. When they asked his mother, she feigned ambivalence, claiming that "she didn't know her sons anymore. After they married, they were no longer her responsibility."

This stands in stark contrast to B.R., whose mother pushed him to surrender, bravely telling the police *not* to shoot him because she knew his character and knew he could come back from this. However, B.R. emerged from the conflict period with his siblings alive and with few, if any, losses among his close family. It is not surprising that Yuda's parents may have been more receptive to their son's desire to exact revenge. Knowing he had the support of his family had hardened Yuda. Even as late as 2012, he stated that if he was let out of jail tomorrow, he would immediately seek to take up arms.

Yuda was sentenced to eighteen years in prison, among the steepest sentences of all the hit-squad members. However, prison was not a time for reflection and reconsideration for him. His time in prison only hardened him further. He saw his life as defined by three pathways. He explained:

> As a *mujahid* [holy warrior], we only have three options: be a fugitive, get arrested, or die. Being a fugitive for us is like a picnic. If we get arrested, it is an opportunity to become closer to Allah. If we are shot dead, we die a martyr. Jail doesn't make us feel down. It doesn't scare us. It inspires us. Jail is the place where we sharpen our fangs. We got sent to jail for killing one infidel, God willing, we will kill ten infidels.

At the time of the interview in Ampana in 2012, Yuda contended that terror actions were still needed in Poso and that he was still committed to exacting revenge.

> I am still vengeful. That desire comes from Allah. Allah tells us to wage war against infidels, wherever you find them. This isn't an order from any [person], not the president [or anyone else]. It comes from Allah. Insyallah, until Allah takes my life, I will carry this revenge.

In April 2013, Yuda's wife was ill, having suffered a miscarriage. He arranged with the officials at the jail to permit him to visit her. For some reason, only one guard accompanied him. After Friday prayers, he slipped away, fleeing into the mountains to join Mujahidin Indonesia Timor (MIT).[3] He lived the life of a fugitive for three years until he was finally arrested again in 2016.

There are several key factors that differentiate Yuda from the other life histories in this book. Unlike B.R. and Ali Imron, he felt no sense of disillusionment regarding the targets of terror attacks; he even felt justified and continues to feel justified in the murder and mutilation of the schoolgirls. Second, unlike B.R., Anas, and Ali Fauzi, at no point did Yuda attempt to expand his social network beyond Tanah Runtuh or, subsequently, those hard-liners in Tanah Runtuh who broke away to form Mujahidin Indonesia Timor. While many of his peers in Tanah Runtuh came to realize, after expanding their social networks, that the context had changed, Yuda's social network within MIT is dedicated to perpetuating violence. Unlike B.R. and Agus (see chapter 2), he did not receive pressure from family members to quit either group. His priorities remain steeped in violence. As a result of his torture at the hands of Densus and the killing of his brothers during the raids, the target of his vengeance has shifted, however, from Christians to the police and security apparatus itself.

8

The Role of the State and Civil Society in Disengagement Initiatives

This book has highlighted the importance of relationships and priority shifts in successful cases of disengagement and reintegration. Rational assessments of costs and benefits, as well as feelings of disillusionment, also contribute as they influence perceptions of current reality for the individual, the group, and the larger community in which they operate. This chapter will analyze programs by the state and civil society that attempt to facilitate disengagement and deradicalization, as well as such efforts within the community of already disengaged jihadists. It will analyze the merits and shortcomings of programs that have already been conducted, highlight best practices, and suggest ways to improve upon those efforts.

Government Programs

Indonesian government efforts to promote cooperation, disengagement, and deradicalization have shifted over the past decade. Initial programs were ad hoc, underfunded initiatives conducted by the police counterterrorism team Detachment 88 (Densus 88) and a few select local governments. These correctly identified the problems and showed a real understanding of their respective contexts, but the solutions were often not well implemented, most often because of insufficient resources and misaligned goals.

In 2010, Densus 88 was incorporated into a new coordinating bureau, the National Counter-Terrorism Bureau (BNPT), which was well staffed and amply resourced. However, disengagement was not given priority, and programs often suffered from a lack of understanding of the target participant group and how best to reach them. Thus, as of 2016, the government role was limited in the fields of disengagement and reintegration, with most programs coming from either civil society or the already disengaged jihadist community. However, there is real room for government actors from the BNPT, the Department of Corrections, and other agencies to work together to encourage disengagement via prison reform, job training, and aftercare initiatives. This section will analyze the initiatives and programs that have taken place over the past decade.

Densus 88 and the Soft Approach

The first attempt at facilitating disengagement of jihadists in Indonesia was an ad hoc initiative begun by Suryadharma, then the head of Densus 88, the police counterterrorism team, and continued by his successor, Tito Karnavian. This off-budget, grossly underfunded effort, known as the "soft approach," made international news for the innovative idea that well-respected senior jihadists who had already disengaged could persuade their subordinates to follow suit through formal and informal discussions.

Key to this initiative were two senior members of Jemaah Islamiyah, Nasir Abas, a Malaysian citizen and the former commander of Jemaah Islamiyah's training region, Mantiqi 3, and Ali Imron, a somewhat reluctant participant in the 2002 Bali bombing. That these two senior JI members agreed to cooperate with Densus in this regard was something of a coup. Although Nasir Abas had not participated in any bombings, he was well respected, having been a trainer at the As Sadaah camp on the Pakistan side of the border during the Soviet-Afghan War, and having set up Camp Hudaibiyah, JI's training camp in Mindanao. He says he opposed Osama bin Laden's 1998 fatwa legitimating the killing of civilians, but he believed in the use of military force to fight against oppression of Muslims. Ali Imron was a highly respected Islamic scholar with jihad experience in Afghanistan and Ambon. He participated in several bombings, including the attack on the Philippine ambassador's residence, the Christmas Eve bombing, and the first Bali bombing. He took a different view from that of Abas, contending that the bombers' interpretation of jihad was actually correct but they had acted precipitously, without assessing whether they had popular support, the necessary strength to take on the state, and a secure base from which to mount operations, whether the Muslim community would benefit from their actions, or whether they could achieve the same goals via religious outreach.[1] It was this nuanced perspective, among other factors, that convinced key JI figures and contributed to the emergence of JI's dominant anti-bombing-in-Indonesia narrative.[2]

The International Crisis Group explained the program from the perspective of the police as follows:

> The Police took a major gamble in giving [Abas and Imron] access to other detainees to engage in informal debates and encourage discussion about what was right and wrong in their approach to jihad. . . . The Indonesian police understood at the outset that any debates about right and wrong tactics had to take place within the movement itself. Jihadis were not going to listen to moderates from outside their own circle. . . . One goal of the police in giving Ali

Imron and Nasir Abas access to new detainees was to pick off important leaders of JI in the belief that given JI's hierarchical structure, if the leader changed his mind, others would follow.[3]

Within the parameters of this approach, Nasir Abas had the higher profile because he could freely move about the country and meet with jihadists both inside and outside of prison. Ali Imron's scope of influence was largely confined to his fellow terrorist prisoners serving time in POLDA Metrojaya detention center. At the time, however, prominent members of JI and Tanah Runtuh were detained at POLDA, including Abu Dujana, Mubarok, and a good portion of the Tanah Runtuh hit squad. Thus, he too was influential.

In tandem with discussions held by Ali Imron and Nasir Abas, Densus 88 also applied its "soft approach" through humane treatment of prisoners, including interaction and the building of relationships, to undermine the narrative that the police were inhumane and un-Islamic. When Suryadharma was Densus chief, he led prayer sessions in prisons, and interrogation sessions were often stopped for prayers.[4] During Ramadan, Densus members shared the *iftar* (break the fast) meal with the prisoners. On several occasions Suryadharma also took detainees at POLDA for outings to visit orphanages and scavengers to show how one could be a good Muslim and contribute to the welfare of the Muslim community without the use of violence.[5]

Tito Karnavian explained that after studying the background of the arrested jihadist, if he found that the prisoner was amenable to cooperating, he would seek to build a relationship of trust, where in time the detainee would feel comfortable sharing his problems and concerns.[6] Certain jihadists were also singled out for special treatment, if their cases were high priority, if they cooperated with authorities, or if they showed promise. In a handful of instances, for example, Densus allowed jihadists to marry their girlfriends in ceremonies at the detention center, with family flown in for the occasion. Such humane treatment had an impact on certain jihadists. One Tanah Runtuh member who participated in the Tentena marketplace bombing explained how Densus's humane treatment and the conversations he had as part of the soft approach helped him to change his views.

> Initially, I considered [the police] *thogut* [un-Islamic]. However, they treated me humanely, providing food and a bed in POLDA Metro. Initially, I argued that the police had made a big mistake following Indonesian laws [because] they are man-made. I favor Islamic law. However, [I realize] it would be difficult to implement Islamic law in Indonesia because five or six religions are officially regarded. To implement sharia takes time. I now preach Islam patiently because Islam teaches ethics among humans. I have realized that [the police] could not be characterized as *thogut* as I thought. Some Densus members pray, and sometimes we chat with them. I have changed my mind about the police after times of deep reflection.[7]

While interviewees for this research cited the soft approach directly only 16 percent of the time in disengagement narratives, many more cited damage done by the use of torture and the lack of trust in the authorities. The core ideas behind the soft approach, most notably humane treatment, relationship building, and in-group conversations with the already disengaged, were beneficial. The issues with the soft approach lay not in the idea itself, but with improper measurement of success, insufficient resources to build a proper program, and inconsistent enforcement of norms of behavior.

When asked about the success of the soft approach in 2010, Tito Karnavian estimated that of the two hundred prisoners whom

Densus 88 approached, half were cooperative.[8] The language Karnavian used highlights one of the core issues with the program. The soft approach was never actually a disengagement program, irrespective of how it was portrayed in the international media.[9] The top priority of the soft approach was to gather intelligence on Jemaah Islamiyah and its affiliates to better assist in heading off terrorist attacks and to understand the inner workings of the network. In short, the goal was to facilitate cooperation, not reintegration. Disengagement was a positive byproduct, rather than the focal point. The conflation of cooperation with disengagement inhibited Densus from doing systematic analysis of successful cases of disengagement and then building on best practices.

Also, the program was ad hoc, underresourced and underfunded. In contrast to the teams of social workers, religious scholars, and psychologists staffing programs in Singapore and Saudi Arabia, a small subgroup of Densus, together with Nasir Abas and Ali Imron, composed the entirety of the cooperation-cum-disengagement effort. Karnavian lamented the scarcity of resources available for counterterrorism. "The police team has a tiny operating budget. This inhibits the optimum outcome. There are many things that could be done that are beyond our capacity, for example, paying for the school fees for the children of imprisoned radicals or helping their families after imprisonment."[10] Even after a series of meetings in 2007 between the Police Bomb Task Force and twenty-eight Afghan veterans who rejected the use of indiscriminate violence raised the possibility of a life-skills program to help newly released detainees find a way to make a living legitimately, little was done.[11]

Another shortcoming of the soft approach was its inconsistent application. Despite the obvious benefits of humane treatment and its use at the national level at POLDA, and for those who surrendered to the police, it was reported by many of those interviewed that the default behavior of local police and local Densus branches was often torture upon arrest.[12] In repeated interviews, it was stated that those who surrendered were treated humanely, while those who were arrested by the authorities, especially local authorities, faced up to a week of torture at the hands of their interrogators.[13] One young man from Ampana who joined in attacks on Christian villages early in the Poso conflict contended he was tortured so badly that he retained permanent damage to his left eye.[14] Another, a former member of the Subur cell, which assisted Noordin M. Top, described being stripped down to his underpants and beaten.[15] The use of torture led some, who may have been ripe for disengagement, to be susceptible to further radicalization as a result of their treatment at the hands of the police. In the small-scale bombings that took place between 2009 and 2013, police were a frequent target.

Some have expressed skepticism over the soft approach, particularly in emboldening men like Nasir Abas and Ali Imron and giving them a forum for their perspective, which is not a complete renunciation of violence. Susan Sim, vice president for Asia at the Soufan Group, notes that both Abas and Imron adjusted their previous views rather than abandoning them. "They reject violence against civilians, but if you listen to them, they do not reject violence per se. They say, 'Yes, we regret the Bali bombing,' but if you dig down, what they basically say is, 'We regret the tactical errors that JI committed. Next time, we will be prepared and we will attack only from a position of strength.'"[16] She goes on to explain that "they still believe that they have a duty to kill Americans, Israelis, Russians—but soldiers, those who are involved in fighting Muslims in conflict zones."[17]

While the concerns raised by Sim have merit, one has to question whether terrorist detainees would listen receptively to someone with no jihad experience, who preached nonviolence in all circumstances, even in combat zones. Evidence from Sarlito Sarwono's program discussed later in this chapter would indicate the contrary. Sim, a former intelligence analyst in Singapore, is basing her comments on the Singaporean program, which does employ religious teachers who have no jihad experience to deradicalize and resocialize terrorist detainees. However, most of the JI members who joined the Singaporean deradicalization program had played nonviolent roles in JI operations. Those who did not join in a jihad or participate in any violent activities may be open to a comprehensive Singaporean-style approach, especially if it includes a reduced sentence. To reach JI leaders or operatives with jihad or terrorism experience, however, the best results may come from encouraging them, in consultation with their already disengaged seniors and contemporaries, to revise their views on the use of violence, debating questions of implementation, of targets, timing, location, and condition. This does not preclude them from drifting further away from jihad ideology over time, as they leave prison and become more focused on building a post-jihad life.

Local Government Efforts

Contemporaneous with the Densus soft approach, there were also local government reintegration efforts, most notably in the Poso district. In 2007 and 2008, following the Densus 88 raids, two programs were conducted targeting former combatants in Poso. The first, carried out by the provincial police, provided thirty Muslim participants with short courses of vocational training and in-kind business capital assistance.[18] The second was a one-time cash payment of Rp 10 million (US$1,000) to approximately 170 individual Muslim recipients and 90 Christian recipients.[19] The funding

was to help start new businesses. While the ideas were more conducive to supporting reintegration, there were significant flaws in
implementation. First, the programs were too small-scale. Second,
many ex-jihadis who were offered the opportunity to participate in
the job training program were already employed.[20] When the bureaucrats from the agency responsible for designing and running
the program were interviewed, they suggested that key tasks like
participant selection were complicated by small budgets and the
fact that all funds had to be spent during a single fiscal year.[21] There
was insufficient time for careful planning and candidate selection.[22]

Independently, within Poso itself, the local government and police also attempted to assist local jihadis to reintegrate into society by providing connections, start-up money, skills training, and
contract employment. While these activities have been conducted
on an ad hoc basis, the results have been tangibly felt by a wider
array of ex-jihadis. The goal of this endeavor has been to make
them "too busy to fight."[23] However, it has also had the effect of
resocializing some of the Poso jihadists into the larger community,
which has led some who served long prison terms to understand
the implications of Poso having been peaceful for over a decade.
For others, however, it made no difference. By 2010, Poso had become a hub for Jemaah Anshorut Tauhid (JAT), and some Tanah
Runtuh members, who still felt vengeful and wanted to continue
to mount attacks, particularly against the police, joined JAT or
MIT. The existence of these programs and their participation in
them made no difference.

The BNPT

The Indonesian National Counter-Terrorism Bureau (BNPT)
was founded in July 2010, almost a year to the day following the

2009 bombings of the Marriott and Ritz-Carlton Hotels. Its purpose was to coordinate among government agencies in three areas: intelligence gathering, monitoring, and operations; prevention and deradicalization; and international cooperation. Densus 88 was incorporated into the BNPT, which in theory would have provided a wealth of experience upon which to draw. The BNPT, however, has been quite ineffective. According to the Institute for Policy Analysis of Conflict (IPAC), part of the problem at the BNPT is personnel. At the formation of the agency, the military demanded a role and was tasked with prevention *and* deradicalization. Those law enforcement officers with experience, relationships, and direct field knowledge joined the intelligence, monitoring, and operations division, which left prevention and deradicalization to newcomers who lacked experience in those areas.[24]

There were also problems of coordination. Counterterrorism police, who had spent the better part of the past decade building up contacts and gathering information, were reluctant to share it.[25] Had they been freer in sharing their information, it may have helped the prevention and deradicalization division. However, prevention and deradicalization also neglected to do their own research. Had they thoroughly reviewed the interrogation reports and court transcripts, they could have better understood the process of radicalization, and thus both counter-radicalization and disengagement programs could have been better conceived.[26] BNPT has also been reluctant to coordinate with the Department of Corrections (DGC), viewing it as part of the problem, given Indonesia's notoriously corrupt prison system. Yet prison reform would be one component of a comprehensive disengagement effort, which would necessitate such coordination.

On the national level, the military took steps to justify its involvement in the BNPT. Between prevention and deradicalization, the latter has received short shrift. Moreover, the military viewed terrorism through the prism of its organizational identity. A 2011 strategic plan blamed terrorism on a weak sense of nationhood, weak citizenship education, the erosion of local values via modernization, and a fanatic understanding of religion.[27] As the Indonesian military sees itself as the guardian of nationhood, such a perspective validates its own presence, but is at odds with the reality of radicalization as a social experience where kinship ties, teacher-student ties, and the bonds formed in entry-level study circles often are more binding than ideology. Furthermore, it ignores how a politicized local conflict can engender radicalization. This misinterpretation had negative spillover effects on deradicalization program design, as initiatives did not address the needs of the target population or show sufficient understanding of that population.

BNPT deradicalization efforts are frequently criticized as poorly conceived and implemented, disconnected from the actual needs of the target population. In interviews with civil society actors working on disengagement, several common points were raised. First, BNPT programs are too top-down both in organization and in style.[28] Second, BNPT does not perform needs assessments among target populations, to find what types of programs would be best received, before embarking on programming, nor does it examine what programming infrastructure already exists.[29] Third, programs are not sustained over time in a manner that builds trust between the staff and the participants.[30] Fourth, after programs are conducted, BNPT conducts no outcomes assessment to see if there is any change in the participants.[31] Finally, aftercare is still being neglected.[32]

The Wayang Kulit shadow-puppet performances held in prisons in 2011 are an example of this weakness. The planners at BNPT believed that the nonviolence-themed Wayang show would help persuade the terrorists to return to their Javanese heritage. This shows a lack of understanding of the mechanisms behind disengagement and ideological reconsideration. When the terrorist detainees seemed unreceptive to the show, the program was temporarily shelved and later reimagined as a counter-radicalization program for youths, with the same justification.

A more appropriate December 2013 initiative involved bringing in three well-respected hard-line clerics from the Middle East: Ali Hasan al Halabi, a Salafi cleric from Jordan; Dr. Najih Ibrahim, one of the founders of Islamic Jihad in Egypt; and Hisyam al Najjar, a former member of the Jihad Group, who was now active in a Salafi political party.[33] All three opposed violence against civilian targets, as well as the declaration of *takfir* against other Muslims. The three clerics held short courses for terrorist detainees in Cipinang prison in Jakarta and at Pasir Putih prison on Nusa Kambangan island, where some of the most high-risk terrorists are held, in addition to participating in a conference at the University of Indonesia and sitting for a TV interview.[34] While the detainees enjoyed the opportunity to engage the visiting clerics in a lively conversation, the discussion mirrored many points that were already being discussed within the JI community itself. Drawing on the writings of Abu Musab al Suri, who advocated assessing each potential activity undertaken based on its permissibility according to Islamic law, its benefit to the Muslim community and jihad movement, and whether the group possessed the capacities to successfully carry it out, JI leaders had already applied cost-benefit analysis to the terror attacks in Indonesia and decided the costs to the organization were far too high.[35] Many of these same leaders participated in the discussions with the Egyptian and Jordanian clerics. This raises the question of whether the visits actually contributed to disengagement or the reconsideration of previously held views. Rather than bring in Middle Eastern scholars, it may have been better to simply build upon what was already present and encourage these discussions and assessments within the Indonesian jihadist community, both in prison and outside it.[36]

Another program that falls under deradicalization, which has been under discussion since 2011, is a deradicalization center at Sentul. The actual building has already been built, but to date there is no clear plan for its use. The BNPT would like to use the facility as a deradicalization showcase to highlight the most "cooperative" prisoners.[37] The Corrections Directorate, by contrast, would prefer the Sentul facility be used to house the most violent and hard-line extremists.[38] To date, there has been no resolution of this disagreement, and coordination among the various agencies that would be relevant to the center's success is still lacking. In short, the center's evolution seems to have occurred in a reverse order.

There have been some ad hoc, sporadic attempts at life-skills training programs. For example, BNPT officials brought a group of disengaging Islamist extremists together and gave them each a cow. In another instance, "Amru" reported that BNPT directed him to convene a workshop on running a restaurant. However, the subject matter seems to have been decided in an arbitrary, top-down fashion. A better approach would have been to first survey the participants to gauge their areas of interest before setting up workshops. Moreover, workshops need to be ongoing in order to teach various aspects of an occupation.

In short, going back to the initial counterterrorism efforts in the aftermath of the first Bali bombing, disengagement and aftercare have been given short shrift. Early initiatives by Densus 88 established a good base in understanding the jihadists and their needs, but these efforts were ad hoc and underfunded, and humane treatment was inconsistently used. Promising local programs ran into problems of implementation, as higher-ups demanded the funding be used up within a year, which led to a rush to find participants and carry out programs regardless of whether the programs were actually targeting those who needed them most. BNPT's efforts at deradicalization that followed ran into problems of coordination, infighting between the police and military, and a general lack of knowledge as to how to go about the extraordinarily large and difficult job they had been assigned. As a result, Indonesia still does not have an official government-run disengagement program to speak of at the national level. However, it is important to note that the jihadists are still disengaging, irrespective of the degree of assistance they are receiving from the state. Moreover, there are reservoirs of knowledge and expertise within the BNPT, the Department of Corrections, the jihadi community, and civil society that can be tapped to improve upon the initial efforts.

The Porong Model

Specific prisons have also begun to pioneer life-skills training programs, the most notable being a business empowerment program in Porong prison. At Porong, inmates receive small amounts of seed capital to start in-prison businesses. They meet monthly to report on their progress and give 10 percent of their profits back to the prison to fund other activities.[39] Projects have included growing vegetables on the premises and raising ducks and selling them to the prison canteen.[40] Asep Jaja, a former member of Mujahidin KOMPAK serving a life sentence for his role in the 2005 Loki attack, is a key participant in these activities. Such activities complement the efforts of many of the nongovernmental organizations that work with disengaging jihadis in Indonesia, by helping participants develop professional and entrepreneurial skills that may prove useful upon release as they attempt to reintegrate into society. Given the paucity of aftercare programs more generally, such a preparatory program is particularly useful. There is some indication, according to the Institute for Policy Analysis of Conflict's 2016 report, *Update on Indonesian Pro-ISIS Prisoners and Deradicalization Efforts*, that the Porong model is being adopted at other prisons.[41] The generalization of such a program across prisons would aid in facilitating reintegration by providing life skills training and professional development in prison prior to release.

Efforts among Disengaged Jihadists to Facilitate Disengagement and Reintegration

An interesting development outside of prison has been has been the efforts by disengaging jihadists to assist others in disengagement via support groups and opportunities to develop their businesses. The most notable of these has been a mutual aid society established by Ali Fauzi for veterans of the Afghanistan, Moro, Poso, and Ambon conflicts living in his hometown of Lamongan. Lamongan gained a reputation as a hub of radicalism in Indonesia, first for being the hometown of Muchlas, Amrozi, and Ali Imron, three key figures in the 2002 Bali bombing, and more recently for the existence of several pro-ISIS groups within town. Recognizing the need to assist the families of veterans of Afghanistan, Ambon, Poso, and Moro living in Lamongan, Ali Fauzi identified about a dozen families in need of economic support. Their mutual aid activities have included a joint goat-breeding initiative, giving small loans to members facing imminent cash shortages, and an informal religious study group where they could examine their beliefs and explore Islamic law more fully.[42] If a family lacked the funds to pay their children's school fees, Ali Fauzi arranged for the children to attend the al Islam *pesantren* at a heavily subsidized rate. The group also facilitated discussions where individuals with relatives in jail or fighting in Syria could express their views and their needs without fear.[43] The Institute for Policy Analysis of Conflict notes that such economic empowerment helps the wives of detainees become more assertive in sharing their views, including opposition to ISIS.[44] This is important, for, as noted in several cases in this study, particularly from Poso, wives and mothers can have a discernible impact on their husbands' and children's decision to disengage. Perhaps most important, the mutual aid society has provided an alternative social network of sorts for individuals who decide to disengage and become more open in their perspective. They need not fear ostracism from the jihadi community on the whole because the mutual aid society constitutes a set of friends who support their decision. This provides a source of empowerment for facilitating reintegration.

The mutual aid society in Lamongan is an important example of how disengagement and reintegration can be assisted and even facilitated through careful and targeted programming. Moreover, it points to the importance of recruiting the right people with legitimacy among those in the radical community, men like Ali Fauzi, who have the jihad experience and religious training, who can empathize with others' experiences, and who understand the journey on which the men are embarking.

It is too early to assess the ultimate results of such a model. If we go back to the 2007 meeting among the Afghan veterans, the mutual aid society's activities echo the themes raised by the jihadists present about the need for economic empowerment. This points to something perhaps unique in Indonesia: there is a cadre of current and former JI, Tanah Runtuh, and Mujahidin KOMPAK members who still retain links in the form of friendship and kin relations with their radical community but are also engaged in the world outside that community. This can be a potential asset for those involved at the national and local levels in promoting disengagement and reintegration.

Civil Society Initiatives

In addition to government programs and initiatives coming from the disengaging jihadists themselves, we also find several initiatives coming out of local and international civil society. The most notable are Search for Common Ground, the Institute for International Peace Building (YPP), the Institute for Social Empowerment (INSEP), and Sarlito's program. The first three work mainly in development of job training and life-skills building. The last was an attempt at religious reeducation. All are small-scale programs. The first three could be ripe for expansion, if done in a careful and targeted manner. One consensus that has emerged from all these programs is that terrorist detainees do not want to talk religious ideology with outsiders. They are far more open to life-skills training and professional development programs.

Search for Common Ground and INSEP both work in the arena of life-skills training. Search for Common Ground runs a small conflict-management program in prisons and has provided seed money to foster other disengagement-focused organizations, including the Institute for International Peace Building. INSEP also runs programs in prisons offering practical skills training, including air conditioning repair, calligraphy, yogurt making, cooking, and mechanics. Staffed by trained psychologists and social workers, these programs are based on needs assessments, and prioritize interaction rather than simple delivery of information.

According to Zora Sukabdi, former head of reintegration at INSEP, "The program is unstructured. If they want to dialogue, we dialogue. If they want to learn something, we will do it. If they want to study the Quran, we will do it."[45] Sukabdi lauded her program for being innocuous enough on the surface to allow her and her colleagues entry into some of the most resistant prisons and prison populations.

Working closely with the Department of Corrections in eight prisons throughout Indonesia, Search for Common Ground is more specific in its approach. It offers workshops in conflict management for terrorist prisoners in an effort to prevent recidivism. The program is actually a training of trainers, where the terrorist prisoners are taught conflict-management skills that they in turn teach to their subordinates. According to Agus Hadi Nahrowi, the former program manager at Search for Common Ground, who ran many of these programs,

> We focus on high-risk prisoners in Cipinang, Porong, Nusa Kembangkan. We usually have about twenty-five prisoners per session, a combination of terrorist prisoners and other high-risk prisoners like drug dealers. We use an experiential learning model, combining role play, activities, games, and discussion to address topics like the nature of conflict, how one's position and interests may affect their standing in a conflict, how to deal with conflict, how to give empathy, how to build trust, and how to be a peace builder.[46]

Program personnel would visit the prisons on a quarterly basis to see how the terrorist prisoners were using the skills they had learned. In total, Nahrowi estimated, they had trained one hundred terrorist prisoners across the eight targeted prisons. In assessing the success of the program, Nahrowi admitted that low-level prisoners were more receptive than the high-level ones, who tended to be more "judgmental."[47]

A final program of note, which has received significant media attention, is the Institute for International Peace Building. Founded by Noor Huda Ismail, a graduate of the Ngruki Islamic boarding school and a former *Washington Post* journalist, and Taufik Andrie, another former journalist, YPP began as a somewhat ad hoc initiative where Andrie and Ismail reached out to their former journalism sources among the jihadists to see how they could help them to reintegrate successfully. Taufik Andrie explains, "We began with a needs assessment that we conducted between 2006 and 2008, and in 2009 we began formally helping two people to set up businesses with an end goal of facilitating successful rehabilitation."[48] Over its six years in operation, YPP has assisted fifteen people and is monitoring another fifteen to see if engagement is possible after prison.[49] The number is low, Andrie contends, because the process of helping the jihadists is labor intensive.

Andrie explains that their method is a three-step process, and they do not seek out participants; they work with those who seek them out. First, they do research on interested disengaging jihadists to learn as much as possible about their case and their background. Then they approach them to build a relationship, calling on a weekly basis and visiting them once every two months. In doing so, they come to an understanding of the prisoner's goals and needs. Third, they seek to build loyalty and trust in that relationship by fulfilling the prisoner's needs—assisting with children's school fees, for example, and helping the men, upon release, to put together a business plan, find seed capital for a small business, or obtain professional training. This, Andrie contends, can take up to two years. In time, as trust is built, affirmed, and reaffirmed through their rehabilitation program, in certain instances the YPP members may begin to challenge the jihadist's ideas on jihad or the Islamic state.[50]

The YPP "graduates" include stockbrokers, small businessmen, and lecturers. Ali Fauzi was an early participant in YPP's program, prior to the initial needs assessment in 2009. With encouragement from YPP and his brother, he went on to obtain a master's degree from Muhammadiyah University.[51] Another example is "Amru," a former JI member who had fought in Mindanao. He chose to disengage from violence, and after release from prison he approached Noor Huda Ismail for assistance. Together, Noor Huda and Amru set up a hip café, Dapur Bistek, where Amru worked as manager. Amru was approached in 2010 to be a trainer at the Lintas Tanzim training camp in Aceh, but after consideration, he refused, citing the ties of his new life. He explained how working at Dapur Bistek had changed his perspective. "At the restaurant, I have to interact with all types of people, Muslims, Christians, women without headscarves, whomever. I have to serve them all."[52] After a few years, Noor Huda Ismail, Taufik Andrie, and Amru began to discuss ideological issues as well, which shaped Amru's reconsideration of previously held views. Later, they were joined by another disengaging jihadist, who would do the café's finances and later go on to work in business. A third disengaging jihadist gained employment at the Solo branch of Dapur Bistek before striking out on his own.

Andrie says that the greatest challenge for YPP is the image problem it has both among terrorists and with the government. "Subgroups of the terrorists do not like what we do. They think we are bought and paid for by the government. They think our intentions are not pure. There are those in the government who suspect we are terrorist sympathizers. We are neither. We do disengagement. We help them stay away from violence. The people who work with us and continue to work with us may have radical minds, but they won't do any more violence."[53] However, a second issue is maintenance over time. Dapur Bistek Semarang closed in 2013 because of a land issue. Amru became a driver. It is hard for him to make ends meet. This raises the question of how to best assist program graduates.

In order to expand on its model, YPP would need more human and financial resources. To accomplish its goals, YPP has had to work closely with the Department of Corrections and believes in the potential for the DGC to be an ally in disengagement, in contrast to the view of BNPT. However, YPP would also need to conduct regular assessments of success—two years out, five years out—on its participants. Who has successfully developed a new business? Who has reintegrated into the community? How is reintegration measured? Have past colleagues attempted to re-recruit the program participants? Did any accept? For those who refused, what factors empowered them to refuse? For those who returned to terror, why did they do so? How did YPP miss the signs? For those who fail at their initial businesses, how and to what extent does YPP provide assistance?

Attempts at religious reeducation of jihadists in and out of prison by outsiders have largely failed to bear fruit. The late Sarlito Sarwono's effort was one such initiative. Sarlito, several of his colleagues from the psychology faculty at the University of Indonesia, and several faculty from the State Islamic University Syarif Hidayatullah discussed with program participants a book by Muslim scholar Quraisy Shihab, *Kekerasan Atas Nama Agama* (Violence in the name of religion). This program was conducted in Jakarta, Bandung, Lampung, Semarang, Surabaya, Balikpapan, and Poso in multiple iterations, with five to twelve participants for each session.[54] To incentivize participation, attendees were paid a hefty sum of money for their presence at the program. While some of the attendees were willing to reconsider tactical issues like the permissibility of violence in Indonesia, overall the detainees were not amenable to reassessing their basic understanding of jihad or to being "cognitively restructured" by the staff in attendance.[55] After the death of Sarlito Sarwono, the program was taken over by Benny Mamoto, a former police official. This iteration of the program includes a focus on empowering the wives of jihadists and the former prisoners, providing family assistance, and psychological counseling.

In short, most of the actual disengagement initiatives are coming from civil society. They are very small-scale in nature, but they have several points in common. First, prior to any engagement, the program organizers do their research on the participants. Second, they seek to build trust among participants. Third, INSEP and YPP do needs assessment prior to any programmatic approach. Fourth, they focus on professional development and life-skills training, avoiding ideological hot-button topics. Finally, all use active learning approaches. INSEP and YPP work via learn-by-doing. Search for Common Ground uses experiential learning and discussion. These also echo the themes from the Porong program with Asep Jaja and Ali Fauzi's mutual aid society. These commonalities can be considered as best practices and be instructive for BNPT, Densus, and local government agencies as they attempt to improve upon their own initiatives or start new ones.

The Need for Aftercare Initiatives

One area where BNPT, Indonesian government agencies, civil society, and Islamic organizations could make great strides in coordinating their efforts is in the field of aftercare. Post-release assistance in the initial years can be helpful. Irrespective of how cooperative individual jihadists are in prison, how well behaved they are, they are far more likely to remain disengaged if they are welcomed back into their families and neighborhoods and are able to secure and maintain gainful employment. This offers opportunities for BNPT to coordinate with relevant government departments at the provincial and local levels, and for Islamic organizations and nongovernmental organizations to institute programs, improve upon past efforts, and expand existing programs that show promise.

One part of aftercare deals with monitoring. Sidney Jones, director of the Institute for Policy Analysis of Conflict, explains that the provincial-level office of the Ministry of Law and Human Rights (BAPAS) is charged with doing background research on the prisoner and his family and the community into which he will return, prior to the approval of parole.[56] A parolee on conditional release is then responsible for checking in with his parole officer at BAPAS once a month for the remainder of the sentence, whereas there is no such requirement for someone who completes his full term.[57] According to Jones, this requirement is inconsistently enforced for the conditional release parolees.[58] This is one area for improvement. Effective post-release monitoring can assist in preventing violence.[59] However, BAPAS must also be careful in its monitoring efforts to respect the rights of newly released prisoners to build new lives. Anas criticized those who monitor for being heavy-handed, dropping by the home of newly released prisoners without using discretion and in so doing attracting unnecessary attention to the family.[60] A balance must be struck where monitoring is done effectively and regularly but in a respectful manner.

Another part of aftercare is the development of life-skills and job training. INSEP, YPP, Search for Common Ground, and Ali Fauzi's mutual aid society offer such programs on a small scale, but their efforts are insufficient to address the sheer need. If jihadists cannot find ways to take care of their financial needs independently of the jihadist groups, they are more likely to seek help from these groups. This requires building relationships when they are in prison, much as Densus 88 members did at POLDA, and in so doing, learning about the prisoners' backgrounds and their concerns for themselves and their families. It may require using financial assistance to help facilitate relationships, with those who are willing to participate. Small moves like paying for children's school fees can build loyalty. As the time for release draws closer, providing life-skills and job training would assist jihadists in reintegrating. This points to the importance of expanding the Porong model into prisons throughout Indonesia and offering more areas where one could gain life-skills training. In Poso, where community stigma toward ex-prisoners is less, and government contract jobs, facilitated by the local government, are available, it has been easier for detainees to return to their communities. Local government agencies in other areas may be able to offer similar contract projects or, at the very least, job training so that the ex-prisoners could become eligible to compete for them.

A third part of aftercare is a resocialization, not only for jihadists returning to society, but for the communities and families to which they return. Taufik Andrie notes that some jihadists are rejected by their families when they return from prison, which alienates them from a key set of relationships that preceded any involvement in jihadist activities.[61] Anas explained that disengaged jihadists face stigma in the communities in which they return or settle, if their former identity is found out.[62] At the national level, government agencies working on disengagement and reintegration could perhaps improve this environment by striking the right chords in their speeches when referring to the release of jihadist prisoners.

There could possibly be a role for existing civil society organizations like INSEP, which is run by social workers and psychologists, in helping to rehabilitate these family ties. There is a real need for an actor to play such a role.

A key participant in such a socialization project could be Muhammadiyah, as there is a subset of jihadists who come from Muhammadiyah families. Ali Fauzi noted that when he studied for his bachelor's degree at Muhammadiyah University, he reconnected with his Muhammadiyah roots and came to see his own views as more in line with the mass organization. Another ex-fighter, this one from Central Sulawesi, who also attended a Muhammadiyah University, returned to what he had learned in Muhammadiyah as he was working through the mental processes of disengagement. Muhammadiyah has views similar to those of Salafis on *tauhid* or divine oneness of God. Thus, there may be a special space for Muhammadiyah in disengagement and aftercare, especially if targeted to those "lost" members who grew up in Muhammadiyah families. It is worth noting that Muhammadiyah members are already participating in existing civil society disengagement and reintegration initiatives as social workers and psychologists.

Moreover, the Ma'arif Institute, a Muhammadiyah-affiliated think tank, has been working on counter-radicalization since 2007, with several ambitious projects. Within its own schools in three provinces—West Java, Central Sulawesi, and East Nusa Tenggara—between 2007 and 2010, it provided approximately 150 religious teachers from 150 Muhammadiyah high schools with training in understanding the values of human rights.[63] The institute estimates the benefits of the program reached eight thousand students over the course of the three years.[64] In 2011, after two studies revealed that students were being radicalized by religious teachers in public high schools, the Ma'arif Institute created an antiviolence and character-building education program in public high schools in four cities: Solo, Yogyakarta, Cianjur, and Pandeglang.[65] While the implementation did not go smoothly, particularly in Cianjur, where they were refused entry into certain schools, the Ma'arif staff contend that in time they were able to build relationships with appropriate authorities to allay suspicions. They trained approximately one hundred religious teachers from fifty schools and estimate that some twelve thousand students reaped the benefits.[66] In 2014, Ma'arif staff held a series of workshops for activists from Rohis, an Islamic extracurricular study group, as well as head teachers and heads of schools, first in Yogyakarta and Cianjur and then Java-wide, echoing many of these same themes of universal Islamic values and character building.[67] An estimated four hundred people participated. If the numbers pertaining to student spillover effects bear out, this would be the most successful counter-radicalization program among Indonesian youth. Importantly, this is not coming from BNPT; it is coming from Muhammadiyah, the second-largest Islamic organization in Indonesia and a natural partner in these efforts. In any case, it must be stressed that Muhammadiyah has already carved out a role for itself in counter-radicalization, and Muhammadiyah members in disengagement efforts. That role could be expanded. Muhammadiyah could potentially have value in assisting jihadists in creating their post-jihad identity.

IN ASSESSING DISENGAGEMENT initiatives in Indonesia, it is clear that they are arising from three sources: the government, the already disengaged, and civil society. Whereas programs conducted by civil society and the disengaged, though small scale, seem to be yielding some positive results, the government initiatives have fallen short. We can understand why by contrasting the common methodologies of the civil society programs and the efforts of the already disengaged with those of the government.

Among the civil society actors and the already disengaged, programs begin with needs assessments; they are focused on skill building and professional development; they take time to build trust among participants; and they use active-learning and learn-by-doing methodologies. The sum total of these programs is geared toward aftercare and reintegration. Moreover, discussions of religious ideology are done only after trust is built or by someone well respected from the community itself. When Densus 88 utilized the soft approach, allowing the already disengaged Ali Imron and Nasir Abas to lead formal and informal discussions, its efforts were met with success.

An examination of BNPT efforts, however, shows that these practices are not being implemented. Instead, programs lack needs assessments or outcomes assessments. There is a lack of research done on their target population, despite the availability of data. BNPT overrelies on lecture methods and top-down programs. Interestingly, however, BNPT is seeking the help of Ali Fauzi, Ali Imron, and other disengaged jihadists. It would further benefit BNPT to seek their advice on program design, rather than simply engage them as presenters. It would also be advisable to prioritize disengagement, reintegration, and aftercare as an end in itself.

Conclusion

In April 2015, ISIS defector Ahmed Junaidi was interviewed by the *Jakarta Post*, after having returned home from Syria.[1] He joined ISIS because he felt a sincere desire to help oppressed Muslims and envisioned himself joining in humanitarian relief efforts. It helped that the recruiter promised to repay all his debts, which were substantial, and on top of that spoke of a generous salary. Thus, his motives for joining were both altruistic and material. Following his arrival in Syria, after several weeks of ideological indoctrination and paramilitary training, he was assigned to a unit ordered to guard a remote village. His hopes for participating in humanitarian relief evaporated; he had no say in his responsibilities. He quickly became disillusioned by the monotony of his days spent guarding, reading the Quran, and cleaning the house that he shared with twelve other men. The promised high salary turned out to be a pittance. He was allowed to call his wife only once a month, and each time he did, she asked, "When are you coming home?"[2] He thinks she sensed his depression. He admits, "I felt sick and tired of it all."[3] Not long after the interview, he was arrested for having gone to Syria.

As more young men who served with ISIS return, it is important to develop a comprehensive counterterrorism strategy for dealing with returnees and with different types of returnees. This includes an assessment of any prior violent acts by the individual in question, of whether he would continue to be a threat domestically, or whether he intends to disengage from violence and reintegrate into society. It would require an understanding of the person's reasons for returning home; if he feels any disillusionment toward ISIS and the source of that disillusionment; what resources he has to help him reintegrate; and, if there are no such resources, what would be required to help facilitate that reintegration. Women who have traveled to the Syrian-Turkish border to join family already in ISIS-held territory, only to be turned back by the Turkish authorities, or returning to Indonesia solo may also need assistance tailored to their specific circumstances. A version of the Danish model providing job training and housing assistance may be useful here. Likewise, children and adolescents who return may need programming especially targeted to their needs, with trauma counseling and education provided on site—as Pakistan has done with its Sabaoon program, with the eventual goal of "graduation."

There are several takeaway messages from this book that can help with these efforts. These messages highlight the gradual nature of disengagement; the proper place of disillusionment and cost-benefit considerations; the importance of relationships; and the appropriate role of the state.

Don't Rush Disengagement

True disengagement occurs gradually and incrementally over months and years; successful reintegration takes even longer. For a majority of the jihadists examined in this study, the pathway to disengagement began with either creeping feelings of disillusionment or the growing conviction that the costs of terror attacks were outweighing potential benefits. In this environment, some responded to these feelings by seeking out information on the Quran's rules of war or on the causes of a particular communal conflict. Others became open to new friendships, not necessarily as a source of information or a consciously different perspective, but just for companionship—something different. It is important to note that among those who felt disillusioned or came to the realization that the costs of attacks were too high, this does not mean that they halted all participation upon that realization. Many ignored their feelings and inclinations, continuing to participate in acts of terrorism or in activities in support of terror attacks, such as surveillance, robbery, and bomb building.

In time, however, especially among those who disengaged via departure from the movement, they each came to a tipping point, where they could no longer justify their continued participation in the violent actions or in the group. For B.R., this occurred when he chose to flee to A.B.'s house, rather than go into hiding with his fellow members of Tanah Runtuh. Anas contends he was "finished" when he proved to Aman Abdurrahman that by the irrationality of his argument, all his lawyers were *kafir*. Anas had become alienated by the *takfiri* perspective; he was done. For Ali Fauzi, discussing the Bali bombing with Ali Imron enabled him to resolve his misgivings about it and set a course forward. For Ali Imron, who had held his own private reservations in regard to bombing attacks, his decision to physically move his cell to a different part of the prison, away from his brothers, constituted his way of saying that he was different from his elder siblings and he finally trusted his own convictions. For Agus, the tipping point seemed less like a critical juncture and more like a cascade of information, which he learned first from conversations with Christian fighters in prison in Ambon and then from officials who visited the prison. He realized he had not been involved in a glorious battle of Muslims versus Christians; instead he had been a pawn in a political plot.

After these periods of reflections ultimately reached a decision point to disengage, reintegration was often delayed by the need to serve prison sentences, which presented their own set of challenges. Since most Indonesian prisons are gang-ridden, jihadists felt the need to stick together. After prison release, one must figure out how to reintegrate into society. Those who found they were accepted by their families and pre-jihad friends, who were helped by the Institute for International Peace Building, or who went back to school had more success in reintegrating, as they found an alternative community. In Poso, those who became contractors working on local government projects also had more success than those who were unemployed; and those whose spouses and parents pushed them to "focus on the needs of the family" were less likely to join alternative jihadi groups like Mujahidin Indonesia Timor (MIT).

Three Steps toward Reintegration

Disillusionment and cost-benefit considerations are necessary conditions for disengagement, but they are not sufficient, in themselves, to facilitate reintegration.

More than half those interviewed expressed disillusionment with the use of terror tactics. Specifically, they felt unease or disappointment with the use of bombings and other forms of indiscriminate violence outside of legitimate zones of conflict and in Indonesia. Those interviewed from the founding generation of JI members, specifically the veterans of the Soviet-Afghan War, also expressed disappointment with specific leaders who they felt hijacked the movement or whom they saw as too weak to prevent others from doing so. The younger generation of disengaging jihadists from Jemaah Islamiyah, Tanah Runtuh, and Mujahidin

KOMPAK directed their feelings toward their direct and immediate seniors and mentors.

Over time, in cases where an individual participated directly in an action, an externally directed unease with an action became internalized as a personal sense of remorse for the individual's own role. This may have begun as a nagging feeling that something was not right, a sense of foreboding, or pangs of guilt. Over time, it too progressed into outright regret. For B.R., for example, when he assassinated the prosecutor, it did not feel right. He had tried to avoid participating in the operation altogether, claiming he forgot to bring a weapon, but when his commander produced a gun for him, he lacked the courage to follow through on his convictions. At the trial in 2009, upon meeting the prosecutor's wife, he openly expressed remorse and asked for forgiveness. Ali Imron described a similar situation, where he knew the Bali bombing was wrong—the target was improper—and he tried to persuade his older brother, Muchlas, to abandon the idea. When Muchlas expressed his continued commitment to the operation, however, Ali Imron pushed aside his internal misgivings and followed through as a dutiful soldier. By the time of his arrest, his confidence in his own perspective was beginning to grow. He decided to cooperate and expressed his genuine remorse to the victims.

Of those interviewed, a majority cited disillusionment as one factor in their disengagement process, but there were no instances where disillusionment by itself led to disengagement, even when multiple forms of disillusionment were present. First, as noted earlier, disengagement is a gradual and often nonlinear process. Thus, interviewees cited feeling disillusioned at one point in time, only to push it out of their minds or to rationalize their behavior using arguments from seniors who justified violent attacks. Second, even feelings of intense foreboding gave way to the obligation to obey one's seniors, *sami'na wa atho'na*. In iterated narratives, operatives subordinate their private convictions about the rightness or wrongness of an action to the duty to hear and to obey. Importantly, this does not mean they lack the understanding of right and wrong. Repeatedly, interviewees cited nagging feelings that a target was wrong—the victim or victims were innocent people. Yet those feelings were insufficient to enable them to break away at that time.

Disillusionment and cost-benefit assessment taken together, however, reinforced one another and emboldened individuals in the courage of their convictions. The rational assessment of cost and benefit was mentioned by more than thirty interviewees and was the top-cited factor among those who disengaged but chose to remain in the movement. Rational assessment occurred on many levels. In regions affected by communal conflict, most notably Poso, rational assessment was an evaluation of the current context and conditions versus those during wartime. Of the Tanah Runtuh members, the realization that the context had changed was key to their disengagement. They had two choices: they could join a jihadist group like MIT and continue to wage terror attacks, or they could get jobs, get married, and contribute in some way to the rebuilding of Poso. Respondents from Java-based Jemaah Islamiyah and Mujahidin KOMPAK spoke of the practical and religious reasons why the use of terrorism at this juncture was "counterproductive." Violence against civilians ran counter to the Quran's rules of war. They were too weak at this time to take on the state. The public backlash against terrorism showed that this method would never lead to their winning the hearts and minds of the masses for their cause.

The interaction effect between disillusionment and cost-benefit analysis added weight to those original emotional convictions both through the reflective process and through discussions among groups of disengaging jihadists. That the cost-benefit discussions were already taking place within JI circles legitimized these viewpoints and further encouraged that shift away from the violent factors and splinters. Moreover, as these conversations were already taking place within the group, someone who was disillusioned with terror attacks and who had rationally assessed them to be disadvantageous would not feel required to leave the group or to distance himself from the group. Thus, disillusionment and cost-benefit considerations were indeed sufficient to engender disengagement, but it was a disengagement within the parameters of the network. There was little, if any, evidence of reintegration.

Building an alternative social network, composed of friends, supportive family members, and mentors, is the linchpin of successful disengagement and reintegration.

Just as participation in a radical group is a social experience, so too is there a social component to disengagement and reintegration. When an individual joins a radical group, especially one like Jemaah Islamiyah, which has an extensive induction process, or one like Tanah Runtuh, where members were brought together by a common trauma, the shared experiences of indoctrination, religious study, paramilitary training, fighting in "legitimate" jihads, and participation in terror actions in capacities large and small create social bonds. When individuals join a clandestine movement, they adopt its mental models for understanding a situation, its moral code, and its groupthink. The more involved one becomes in an extremist group, the deeper the social bonds that develop and the more difficult it becomes to give due weight to one's own internal moral code. Furthermore, individuals become bonded by their participation in jihads in what they ascertain are legitimate fields of battle. Agus, Ali Fauzi, and Anas all noted the spiritual component in their participation in jihad and its addictive qualities. From the indoctrination he received regarding jihad, Anas felt as though the angels were smiling down on him and taking note of his actions, while Agus and Ali Fauzi became infatuated with martyrdom. The power of these experiences and the friendships formed as a result were sufficient that Agus abandoned his internal sense of cost and benefit, left his family, and joined the attack on the police post at Loki.

Given the strengths of the in-group attachments, successful disengagement and especially reintegration are far more likely when a jihadist constructs an alternative social network of friends, mentors, and colleagues outside his jihadi community. New friends and relationships offer alternative perspectives. They challenge previously held views. They facilitate priority shifts and open the door to new opportunities. The relationship between A.B. and B.R. between 2005 and 2009 offered B.R. an alternative analysis on the Poso conflict, with A.B. providing a Marxist economic lens for the conflict to contrast with the ideological Muslim-versus-Christian lens that dominated the Tanah Runtuh community. When it came time for B.R. to flee, the strength of the relationship between him and A.B. provided him a refuge not only to disengage from violence but also to separate from his group members and discern his own independent perspective on the Poso conflict. After his release from prison, his re-embrace by his pre-conflict friends emboldened him to begin to construct a post-jihad identity as a musician and a small businessman.

New friends and especially mentors can facilitate a priority shift and help the jihadist conceptualize his post-jihad identity as a contractor, professor, student, stockbroker, small businessman, etc. New friends and relationships can help the jihadist navigate which perspectives he will revise and which he might abandon. As a result of his participation in the field trips from prison arranged by Suryadharma, Anas came to visualize how he could contribute to the Muslim community through social entrepreneurship. Pressure from Noor Huda Ismail, as well as from his brother Ali Imron, convinced Ali Fauzi to go back to school to obtain a degree in Islamic education from Muhammadiyah University. His intensive study during his coursework and the support of his teachers prompted Ali Fauzi to reconsider many of his previous views. This experience contributed to his decision to start his mutual aid society and be a mentor to others who are disengaging, by providing opportunities for group study and discussion where people could reassess their views in a safe space among friends. Even business relationships were shown to have a small impact in strengthening commitment to disengagement and facilitating reintegration. Amru, the former manager at Dapur Bistek, noted that his work at the restaurant challenged him, for he had to socialize with everyone. It did not matter if customers were Christian or Muslim, or wearing an *abaya* or a miniskirt. He had to serve them all. Likewise, several Poso jihadists who subsequently became contractors reported that relationships with other contractors caused them to truly process the extent to which Poso had changed from the conflict period.

This book also found a reinforcing dynamic between new relationships and priority shifts. This was noted by both the Institute for International Peace Building and the Poso jihadists. Gainfully employed jihadists were more likely than unemployed or underemployed ones to feel they were "too busy to fight." Building a business required commitment to its success and created its own social ties; one might well not reengage in radical groups simply because it would alienate new friends at work.

Familial relationships were also important in disengagement. In most instances in this study where familial pressure to disengage came to light, the pressure was from parents. In a small handful of instances, it was a sibling or a spouse. This was particularly true in cases where radicalization was a result of local conflict. B.R.'s mother's efforts to keep her son away from the fighting at critical junctures, like the 2007 Densus raids, likely saved his life, and his knowledge that she was praying for him to surrender gave him crucial emotional support when he finally decided to do so. Of all the factors in B.R.'s lengthy narrative, he says his mother's persistence was the most important in influencing his disengagement. Anas's parents' appeal to Suryadharma to allow their son to leave the prison to finish a second bachelor's degree was crucial to giving him an outlet to reimagine himself, post-prison, as a professional. In other instances, a spouse's appeal to prioritize the family now that the conflict was over led the jihadist to recommit to his family.

In cases where someone remained ideologically and methodologically radical or became a recidivist, however, there was a pronounced lack of alternative social relationships or solidarity with the already disengaged. Yuda kept largely to his jihadi cohort in Ampana prison, and following his escape, he fled into the mountains to join another jihadist group. He professed to have the support of his family in his continued activities. He had no interest in disengaging, and his relationships reflected that. While Reza was a less drastic example, he too was a product of his relationships. Although Reza broke away from KOMPAK head Abdullah Sunata, he actually expanded his radical network through his gun-running business, coming into contact with a wider array of militant groups than he likely would have otherwise.

In short, individuals are more likely to be successful in disengaging from violence and reintegrating into society if they have built an alternative social network of friends, mentors, and colleagues and have the support of their family. They are most likely to be successful in those cases where these friendships and relationships reinforce a priority shift toward family, employment, and furthering their education. The converse is also true. Individuals are more likely to return to terror or remain ideologically and methodologically radical if they keep to a narrow spectrum within the jihadi circle that shares their violent perspective and if they have the support of their parents in continued violence.

If the state builds on the best practices of civil society and works methodically, it has the potential to become a positive player in disengagement and reintegration.

The findings of this book indicate that Indonesia would benefit from creating a holistic approach to counterterrorism, one that recognizes the linkage between prevention and disengagement. If the priority is shifted from preventing the next attack to a more holistic approach of ensuring Indonesia's continued peace and security, then successful disengagement and reintegration of Islamist extremists becomes a critical part of that. This opens the door to thinking creatively about a host of options derived from best practices both in Indonesia and abroad.

First, going back to the era when Suryadharma was head of Densus 88, the ad hoc effort he put forward emphasized understanding the target population and building a relationship with the newly arrested jihadists to show them that the police were indeed not un-Islamic, that the government was not their enemy, and that they could improve the lives of Muslims through nonviolent methods. The emphasis on relationship building was largely abandoned when the BNPT took over. The evidence presented in this book regarding the disengagement process would suggest a return to a focus on relationship building. The initial step in building relationships is to understand the context and the motivations of the jihadists. This requires reading the jihadist dossiers to understand the big picture and to discern key patterns: flashpoints, relationships, and sites of radicalization and recruitment (specific mosques, schools) on a macro level. The next step is to understand the personal story of those jihadists under the state's purview. This will inevitably take time. However, as we saw from when Densus 88 ran programs, it is possible to build those relationships through humane and civil treatment and shared experiences.

Second, those working on disengagement need to take the time to understand the viewpoints of the jihadists and their motivations. There is a mistaken impression among the military men who lead the prevention and deradicalization division in the BNPT that terrorists simply suffer from a deficit of nationalism. The corrective, in their view, is reindoctrinating them in Pancasila, culminating in a signed statement recommitting themselves to the Indonesian nation. There is no evidence that forcing jihadists to sit through lectures on nationalism successfully facilitates disengagement or reintegration, although someone seeking early release from prison may go through the motions of being rehabilitated back into nationalism. Instead, it can be alienating, as jihadists in attendance feel they are being condescended to, rather than being treated with a measure of respect and understanding. The Institute for Policy Analysis of Conflict recommends that the BNPT analyze the arguments the jihadists themselves are making against the use of violence in order to identify the ones most convincing to that community.[4] This is an excellent point. When JI members have held their own discussions regarding *takfir* or the permissibility of the use of violence in certain contexts, arguments against violence have been better received than they would be coming from outsiders. For example, when Ali Imron and Nasir Abas were permitted to hold discussions with other JI leaders regarding the permissibility and utility of violence, this contributed to a shift in the broader JI narrative regarding the use of violence. It would make sense to provide venues both in prison and outside it where these kinds of critical conversations can take place. They are, in fact, already occurring outside of prison, as current and former members of JI who reject ISIS are coming together in public discussions and at book launchings to denounce ISIS and its *takfiri* ideology.

Third, it is important to keep track of the success points in pre-existing disengagement programs. In 2007, Densus 88 brought twenty-seven disengaging Afghan veterans together in Puncak and asked them how the government could best help with the disengagement and reintegration of their fellow jihadists. Life-skills training emerged as one important area where work could be done. Civil society groups like the Institute for International Peace Building (YPP) and the Indonesian Institute for Social Empowerment (INSEP) have run small-scale life-skills training programs, with YPP's efforts focusing more on post-prison release professional development and INSEP running life-skills training workshops for prisoners. Porong prison has also pioneered its own life-skills training program, offering its detainees training in animal husbandry and farming. However, all these programs have been small in scale, and any success has been commensurately small.

Life-skills training and professional development, properly done, can benefit disengaging jihadists by helping them gain employment. First, it is important to ensure that life-skills training and professional development programs be targeted toward those who are already thinking about disengagement. Second, in order to develop appropriate professional development programs, the authorities should conduct needs assessments among their target population and outcomes assessments following the program's conclusion. It makes little sense to offer a professional development program on yogurt making or cow fattening, for example, if your target population is interested in motorcycle or computer repair.

This would likely require a fundamental rethinking at the national level of how these programs are done. Currently, BNPT programs are carried out in a top-down manner. For life-skills training and professional development programs to be successful, they would likely have to be done in a bottom-up fashion, as the needs of disengaging jihadists in Lamongan, for example, would differ from those in Poso, which would differ still from those in Jakarta. Doing these programs at the local level would make it easier to target them appropriately, because there are civil society organizations in these areas with preexisting relationships with the community.

Life-skills training and professional development programs have been shown to assist in reintegration in cases from Denmark to Pakistan. Pakistan's Sabaoon initiative is based on the premise that having a job, a place to go each day, and responsibilities to one's colleagues are far more effective deterrents to recidivism than deradicalization initiatives that attempt to restructure one's thought processes.[5] The program, targeting young men, provides them with education, psychological counseling, training, and job placement. Denmark has also chosen to go this route with returnees from ISIS; those eligible are given assistance in finding a job, housing, and furthering their education.[6] Poso jihadists reported that recidivist friends stayed out of trouble once they obtained gainful employment. They were now focused on their jobs. When life-skills training programs are improperly targeted, they are less successful in encouraging reintegration. In Colombia, for example, "ex-combatants received technical training (in computers, for example) that was not in accordance with the labor demands of the regions to which they returned."[7] Not surprisingly, they were unable to put their new training into practice.

Alongside life-skills training and professional development, there are many small things the government can do to facilitate reintegration. For example, it is currently very hard for newly

released jihadist to obtain ID cards. However, ID cards are critical to life in Indonesia. To help ensure successful reintegration,
post-prison infrastructure is needed. Solving the ID card issue is
one step. Another could be for the ministry of education to offer
a handful of scholarships for those jihadists who want to return
to school to obtain a degree. There is a role for social workers and
counselors in helping to rebuild family ties. In many cases, jihadists
become estranged from their families while in prison. However, it
has been shown in this book and in cases internationally that militants are more likely to successfully disengage and reintegrate into
society when they have a family to return to that supports them.
Moreover, when jihadists return to their home communities, they
may face stigma for having gone to jail or having been part of a
jihadist group. There are ways to ameliorate this. Notably, when
BAPAS or other law enforcement agencies visit neighborhoods
to monitor the progress of newly released jihadists, discretion is
beneficial. Ongoing monitoring can identify who is successfully
reintegrating, who is not making ends meet, who is falling back
onto the wrong path. It is important that groups working with
disengaging and reintegrating jihadists keep up relationships and
monitoring. Someone unable to make ends meet may slowly slide
back into his prior life. As JI is now resurgent and recruiting, new
opportunities will present themselves via old friendships. Thus,
communication channels must be kept open, and aftercare and
counseling options must be available not just for those who start
new businesses immediately post-prison, but also for those who
have failed and are trying to figure out what to do next.

In short, the results of this book point to several ways the Indonesian authorities in conjunction with civil society groups can assist
in reintegration. First, it is imperative to do the research necessary
to understand the target population, their backgrounds, and their

motivations. Second, it is advisable to work *at the local level* to design life-skills training and professional development programs to enable priority shifts. Third, counseling can help repair damaged familial ties. Finally, ongoing monitoring done *with discretion* can identify who needs help *before* he returns to the jihadi community.

The Disengagement of Extremists Worldwide

When we examine the factors that lead to the disengagement and reintegration of extremists on the worldwide stage, many of these same factors emerge as salient. Perhaps the most common point expressed in individual narratives of disengaging extremists across right-wing, left-wing, nationalist, and Islamist terrorist groups is disillusionment with tactics and leaders of the movement or with peers within the movement and assessments of the costs and benefits of continued participation in violent extremist movements.

Those who leave ISIS, irrespective of whether they continued to believe in the group's ideology, explained their defections in terms of disillusionment with leaders, fellow cadres, and brutal tactics. They noted gross inconsistencies between rhetoric and correct Islamic practice, on the one hand, and actual behavior, on the other, noting that ISIS members raped and "got away with it."[8] ISIS members smoked while punishing nonmembers for smoking, and some cadres even refused to allow widows to observe the four-month-and-ten-day Islamic interval before remarriage. Others became disgusted by the sheer brutality and indiscriminate violence carried out by ISIS; people were tortured, beaten, or killed for the most minor of infractions.[9] Military campaigns were carried out without regard for the lives of innocent civilians living in those areas, resulting in the unnecessary deaths of women and children.[10] Others reported disappointment with their quality of life, the corruption of their leaders, and the fact that they never seemed to be targeting the Assad regime in their attacks.[11] These factors contributed to the decision among ISIS defectors to risk leaving the group and returning to their home countries. However, when they do return home, how is reintegration best facilitated? Danish psychologists and social workers have set up a program to facilitate reintegration of Danish ISIS defectors by providing counseling, opportunities to further one's education, and help with housing and employment. Education and employment are key to priority shifts. Importantly, in going back to school and finding a job, one can make new friends. Providing housing ensures a roof over one's head and that basic needs are met. This may be a pathway for Indonesia to consider for its nonviolent ISIS returnees, especially the more than one hundred mostly women and children who were arrested in Turkey without ever crossing the border.

If we turn to the disengagement and reintegration of militants from groups with a longer time horizon, irrespective of whether the individuals in question were members of racist terrorist groups, nationalist terrorist groups, leftist terror groups, or Islamist terror groups, new relationships and priority shifts were important factors propelling these individuals toward disengagement, commitment to that disengagement, and eventual reintegration. While cost-benefit assessments and state inducements most certainly played a role in the decision by the al Gamaah al Islamiyah leadership to revise their views on the use of violence, so too did conversations with Egyptian democracy activist Syed Eddin Ibrahim. Similarly, the willingness of members of the Armée Islamique du Salut to engage with Islamists and non-Islamists outside their circle, especially the Egyptian branch of the Muslim Brotherhood, was an important supporting factor in their decision to demobilize and disarm, for it helped them to reassess previously accepted views.[12] Like members of Tanah Runtuh, disengaging members of the Euskadi ta Askatasuna, the Ulster Volunteer Force, and Scandinavian skinhead gangs all highlight the role of family in encouraging them to cease participation in acts of violence.[13] Moreover, the desire to become a father or, after prison, to be a better father facilitated a critical priority shift to focusing on finding a job and attending to the needs of a family.[14]

The factors found in the Indonesian experience carry over into other terrorist groups, regardless of region or ideological affiliation. Individuals who disengage from violence are likely to experience disillusionment with tactics, leaders, or peers within the movement. They may become disgusted with indiscriminate killing, remorseful for their role in it, or disappointed in leaders who act hypocritically, whose behavior doesn't match their rhetoric. Assessments of the context and the costs of continued violence factor in, especially in group-level and faction-level disengagement, but also at the individual level. However, in the Indonesian case, the development of an alternative social network is especially critical, perhaps because the Indonesian jihadist community is so factionalized. There is always a more violent group to join, always a new opportunity to reengage. However, there is also a strong anti-bombing wing within the Indonesian jihadist community that has postponed the "revolution" until a time when they are "ready," which rejects indiscriminate use of violence outside of legitimate zones of conflict, and thinks that bombings have been "counterproductive" for the group overall. Thus, one can easily go inactive and retain in-movement friends. Such individuals never really fully leave the Indonesian jihadist community, even if they no longer consider themselves members of the particular group. Thus, to disengage and reintegrate, one must have a counterbalancing support structure of friends, family, and mentors that constitute an alternative set of loyalties.

Notes

Introduction

1. For some of the best of these studies see Mia Bloom, *Dying to Kill* (New York: Columbia University Press, 2005); Martha Crenshaw, *Explaining Terrorism: Causes, Processes, and Consequences* (London: Routledge, 2010); Bruce Hoffman, *Inside Terrorism* (New York: Columbia University Press, 1983); John Horgan, *The Psychology of Terrorism* (London: Routledge, 2005); Nelly Lahoud, *The Jihadis' Path to Self-Destruction* (London: Columbia Hurst, 2010); and Marc Sageman, *Understanding Terror Networks* (Philadelphia: University of Pennsylvania Press, 2004), and *Leaderless Jihad: Terror Networks in the Twenty-First Century* (Philadelphia: University of Pennsylvania Press, 2008).

2. *Takfir* is the act of excommunicating a fellow Muslim through accusations that he or she is abandoning Islam and committing apostasy. Among the jihadists I have interviewed, there is a reluctance to pronounce *takfir* against an individual—what if you are wrong? However, a fringe among them has little hesitation in pronouncing *takfir* against not only an individual but also a Muslim community, a city, a country, or even the global Islamic community. This represents a fringe view among radical Islamist groups and even among terrorist groups and is often shunned.

3. Omar Ashour, *The Deradicalization of Jihadists* (London: Routledge, 2009), 94–102.

4. Diaa Rashwan, "The Renunciation of Violence by Egyptian Jihadi Organizations," in *Leaving Terrorism Behind: Individual and Collective Disengagement*, ed. John Horgan and Tore Bjørgo (London: Routledge, 2009), 21–22.

5. Hardi Ibn Harun, former spokesman, FKAWJ, interview with the author, January 2012, Yogyakarta, Indonesia.

6. Omar Ashour, "Deradicalization of Jihad? The Impact of Egyptian Islamist Revisionists on al Qaeda," *Perspectives on Terrorism* 2:5 (2008): 1.

7. Ibid.

8. Ingvild Magnaes Gjelsvik and Tore Bjørgo, "Ex-Pirates in Somalia: Processes of Engagement, Disengagement and Reintegration," *Journal of Scandinavian Studies in Criminology and Crime Prevention* 1 (2012): 5.

9. John Horgan, "Deradicalization or Disengagement? A Process in Need of Clarity and a Counterterrorism Initiative in Need of Evaluation," *Perspectives on Terrorism* 2:4 (2008): 3–8.

10. Adriana Faranda, interview with Alison Jamieson, as cited in Horgan, *Psychology of Terrorism*, 148.

11. John Horgan, *Walking Away from Terrorism: Accounts of Disengagement from Radical and Extremist Movements* (London: Routledge, 2009), 141.

12. Donatella Della Porta, "Leaving Underground Organizations: A Sociological Analysis of the Italian Case," in Bjørgo and Horgan, *Leaving Terrorism Behind*, 68; Horgan, *Walking Away*, 141.

13. Horgan, *Walking Away*.

14. Bjørgo and Horgan, *Leaving Terrorism Behind*, 40–41; Sulastri Osman, "Jemaah Islamiyah: Of Kin and Kind," *Journal of Southeast Asian Affairs* 29:2 (2010): 167–69.

15. "Amru," former JI vice-chair for Jombang, interview with the author, June 2016, Semarang, Indonesia. Nahdlatul Ulama and Muhammadiyah are Islamic mass organizations active in Indonesia. Nahdlatul Ulama has a membership of fifty million Muslims, while Muhammadiyah has a membership of some thirty million Muslims. Amru is using these groups, which run the majority of Islamic boarding schools and madrasas in Indonesia, as a proxy for the Muslim mainstream. The Salafi movements in Indonesia take a far more literal approach to Islam. They take the Quran, the Hadith, and the jurisprudence from only the first four generations following the death of the Prophet Muhammad as authentic and thus try to adhere to the model set out in that corpus. Most Salafis are quietist, eschewing political parties, elections, rallies, and demonstrations, contending that a precondition for political engagement is the achievement of personal and societal transformation.

16. For some of the best of these studies see Bloom, *Dying to Kill*; Barton, *Jemaah Islamiyah*; Crenshaw, *Explaining Terrorism*; Hoffman, *Inside Terrorism*; Horgan, *Psychology of Terrorism*; Lahoud, *Jihadis' Path*; Sageman, *Understanding Terror Networks*; and Sageman, *Leaderless Jihad*.

17. For the best of these al Qaeda–oriented studies see Fawaz Gerges, *The Rise and Fall of al Qaeda* (London: Oxford University Press, 2011); Nelly Lahoud, "In Search of Philosopher-Jihadis: Abu Muhammad al Maqdisi's Jihadi Philosophy," *Totalitarian Movements and Political Religions* 10:2 (2009); and Nelly Lahoud, *Beware of Imitators: Al-Qa'ida through the Lens of Its Confidential Secretary*, Combating Terrorism Center at West Point report, June 4, 2012.

18. For the best of these ISIS-oriented studies see Jessica Stern and JM Berger, *ISIS: State of Terror* (London: William Collins, 2015); William McCants, *The ISIS Apocalypse: The History, Strategy and Doomsday Vision of the Islamic State* (New

York: Picador, 2016); Mia Bloom, John Horgan, Max Taylor, and Charlie Winter, "From Cubs to Lions: A Six Stage Model of Child Socialization into the Islamic State," *Studies in Conflict and Terrorism*, August 2016: 1–20; Mia Bloom, "Constructing Expertise: Terrorist Recruitment and 'Talent Spotting' in the PIRA, al Qaeda, and ISIS," *Studies in Conflict and Terrorism*, September 2016: 1–21.

19. Audrey Kurth Cronin, "How Terrorist Campaigns End," in Bjørgo and Horgan, *Leaving Terrorism Behind*, 8.

20. Ibid., 55.

21. Ashour prefers to use the term "organizational deradicalization." However, his definition of deradicalization is narrow enough to constitute what others refer to as disengagement. Since I am using Horgan's definition of disengagement, and given the stigma that the term "deradicalization" carries with it in Indonesia, I am going to use the term "organizational disengagement" in this chapter. My apologies to Ashour for the switch in terminology.

22. Omar Ashour, *The Deradicalization of Jihadists: Transforming Armed Islamist Movements* (London: Routledge, 2009), 137–41.

23. Ibid.

24. Ibid.

25. Horgan, *Psychology of Terrorism*; Horgan, *Walking Away*; Tore Bjørgo, "The Process of Disengagement from Violent Groups of the Extreme Right," in Bjørgo and Horgan, *Leaving Terrorism Behind*; Donatella Della Porta, "Leaving Underground Organizations," in Bjørgo and Horgan, *Leaving Terrorism Behind*, 68; Horgan, *Walking Away*; Renee Garfinkel, *Personal Transformations: Moving from Violence to Peace*, US Institute of Peace Special Report 186 (April 2007); Angel Rabasa, Stacie L. Pettyjohn, Jeremy J. Ghez, and Christopher Boucek, *Deradicalizing Islamist Extremists* (Arlington, VA: Rand, 2010); Rogelio Alonso, "Why Do Terrorists Stop? Analyzing Why ETA Members Abandon or Continue with Terrorism," *Studies in Conflict and Terrorism* 34:9 (2011): 696–716; Fernando Reinares, "Exit from Terrorism: A Qualitative Empirical Study on Disengagement and Deradicalization among Members of ETA," *Terrorism and Political Violence* 23:5 (2011): 780–803; Ingvild Magnaes Gjelsvik and Tore Bjørgo, "Ex-Pirates in Somalia: Processes of Engagement, Disengagement, and Reintegration," *Journal of Scandinavian Studies in Criminology and Crime Prevention* 13:2 (2012): 94–114.

26. John Horgan, "Individual Disengagement: A Psychological Analysis," in Bjørgo and Horgan, *Leaving Terrorism Behind*, 27.

27. Ibid., 21.

28. Ibid., 21–22.

29. Bjørgo, "Process of Disengagement," 36.

30. Ibid.

31. Reinares, "Exit," 798; Zachary Abuza, "The Rehabilitation of Jemaah Islamiyah Detainees in Southeast Asia: A Preliminary Assessment," in Bjørgo and Horgan, *Leaving Terrorism Behind*, 193–211.

32. Reinares, "Exit," 783.

33. Garfinkel, *Personal Transformations*, 186.

34. See Della Porta, "Leaving Underground Organizations"; Bjørgo, "Processes of Disengagement"; Horgan, *Walking Away*; Diego Muro, "Counter-Terrorist Strategies in Western Europe: A Comparative Analysis of Germany, Italy, Spain and the UK," EUI Working Paper, 2010; Rogelio Alonso, *Killing for Ireland: The IRA and Armed Struggle* (London: Routledge, 2003); Rogelio Alonso, "Pathways out of Terrorism in Northern Ireland and Basque Country: The Misrepresentation of the Irish Model," *Terrorism and Political Violence* 16:4 (2004); Rogelio Alonso, "Leaving Terrorism Behind in Northern Ireland and Basque Country: Reassessing Anti-Terrorist Policies and the Peace Process," in Bjørgo and Horgan, *Leaving Terrorism Behind*; Alonso, "Why Do Terrorists Stop"; Reinares, "Exit."

35. Abuza, "Rehabilitation," 193–211; Christopher Boucek, "Extremist Re-education and Rehabilitation in Saudi Arabia," in Bjørgo and Horgan, *Leaving Terrorism Behind*, 212–23; Christopher Boucek, Shazadi Beg, and John Horgan, "Opening up the Jihadi Debate: Yemen's Committee for Dialogue," in Bjørgo and Horgan, *Leaving Terrorism Behind*, 181–92; International Crisis Group, "'Deradikalisasi' dan Lembaga Pemasyarakatan di Indonesia" [Deradicalization and Indonesian prisons], *Asia Report* 124 (November 19, 2007); Kristen Schulze, "Indonesia's Approach to Jihadist Deradicalization," *CTC Sentinel* 1:8 (2008); Tito Karnavian, "The 'Soft Approach' Strategy in Coping with Islamist Terrorism in Indonesia," working paper, 2009.

36. John Horgan and Mary Beth Altier, "The Future of Terrorist Deradicalization Programs," *Conflict and Security*, Summer/Fall 2012: 86.

37. Jihadist-Salafis combine the purist tendencies of Salafism with the idea that violence is necessary for societal change. Jihadist-Salafis believe it is permissible to use violence to undermine or destabilize a regime, if that regime is not actively working to implement Islamic law. Greg Fealy and Aldo Borgu, "Local Jihad: Radical Islam and Terrorism in Indonesia," ASPI Strategy Paper, September 2005, 14–15.

38. David McRae, "Reintegration and Localized Conflict," *Conflict, Security and Development* 10:3 (July 2010): 405; Gjelsvik and Bjørgo, "Ex-Pirates."

39. Samuel Mullins, "Rehabilitation of Islamist Terrorists: Lessons from Criminology," *Dynamics of Asymmetric Conflict* 3:3 (2010): 175.

40. John Horgan, "What Makes a Terrorist Stop Being a Terrorist?," *Conversation*, November 18, 2014.

41. Abuza, "Rehabilitation," 193–211.

42. Gjelsvik and Bjørgo, "Ex-Pirates," 28; McRae, "Reintegration," 405.

43. Mareke Dennison, "Reintegrating Ex-combatants into Civilian Life," *Peace and Change* 35:2 (April 2010): 338.

44. Sidney Jones, "Battling ISIS in Indonesia," *New York Times*, January 18, 2016.

45. "The Islamic State and Southeast Asia," IISS Strategic Comment no. 36, November 23, 2016, 198.

46. While I interviewed about a dozen others at various points, these were in the initial phases when I was focused more on participation in government programs and less on the disengagement process. Moreover, a handful of interviews were unsuccessful and as a result have not been included in the fifty.

47. Dave McRae, *A Few Poorly Organized Men* (Sydney: Brill, 2013).

48. Former member of Tanah Runtuh team, interview with the author, July 10, 2014, Palu, Indonesia.

49. Former member of Jemaah Islamiyah, interview with the author, 2011, Jakarta, Indonesia.

50. Former member of the Subur cell, interview with the author, January 2011, Semarang, Indonesia.

51. Sidney Jones, "Inherited Jihadism: Like Father, Like Son," *Australian Financial Review*, July 4, 2007.

52. Ibid.

53. Abdul Rauf, member of Ring Banten, interview with the author, January 2012, Banten, Indonesia.

54. Since 99 percent of all interviewees participated in at least one jihad in either Ambon, Poso, Afghanistan, Mindanao, or Syria, I refer to them as *jihadis* or *jihadists*, as that is their defining commonality.

55. ISIS is now using women in operations in Indonesia. See Adam Harvey, "Indonesia Not Prepared to Deal with Female Extremist, Expert Says," http://www.abc.net.au/news/2017-01-14/indonesia-not-prepared-for-potential-female-terrorists-expert/8181796, January 13, 2017.

1. The Rise, Decline, and Resurgence of Jemaah Islamiyah

1. Sidney Jones, "Briefing for the New President: The Terrorist Threat in Indonesia and Southeast Asia," *Annals of the American Academy of Political Science* 618:69 (2008): 71.

2. Information from Greg Fealy via e-mail, July 14, 2016.

3. Information from Sidney Jones, executive director of the Institute for Policy Analysis of Conflict, via e-mail, July 14, 2016.

4. The national ideology of Pancasila, or Five Principles, consists of belief in one god, humanitarianism, social justice, unity in diversity, and democracy through deliberation and consensus. While there had been a proposal—called the Jakarta charter—to enshrine into Pancasila an obligation for Muslims to obey sharia, this was ultimately rejected.

5. Solahudin, *The Roots of Terrorism in Indonesia: From Darul Islam to Jem'ah Islamiya* (Ithaca, NY: Cornell University Press, 2013), 41.

6. Ibid.

7. International Crisis Group, *Recycling Militants in Indonesia*, Asia Report no. 92, 2005, 2.

8. Solahudin, *Roots*, 52.

9. Ibid., 52–57.

10. Ibid., 75.

11. Indonesian modernist Muslims adhere to an orthodox understanding of Islam, centered on the Quran, Hadith, and the first generations of jurisprudential scholarship (rather than the lengthy corpus of scholarship). They are open to modern education and Western technologies. In the independence era, they were represented in the legislature by the Masyumi Party. Many of Indonesia's modernists are members of Muhammadiyah, a mass organization of some thirty million, as well as smaller modernist organizations like United Islam (Persis) and al Irsyad.

12. Masyumi was banned by Sukarno because it refused to back his decision to move the country away from democracy to "guided democracy."

13. Robert Hefner, *Civil Islam: Muslims and Democratization in Indonesia* (Princeton, NJ: Princeton University Press, 2000), 81.

14. Solahudin, *Roots*, 81.

15. Ibid., 62.

16. Quinton Temby, "Imagining an Islamic State in Indonesia," *Indonesia* 89 (2010): 22.

17. Justin Hastings, *No Man's Land: Globalization, Territory, and Clandestine Groups in Southeast Asia* (Ithaca, NY: Cornell University Press, 2010), 24.

18. International Crisis Group, *Recycling Militants in Indonesia*, 13.

19. Ibid., 12.

20. Hastings, *No Man's Land*, 47.

21. Ibid., 51.

22. Solahudin, *Roots*, 133.

23. Sally Neighbour, *In the Shadow of Swords: How Islamic Terrorists Declared War on Australia* (Sydney: HarperCollins, 2004), 85.

24. Solahudin, *Roots*, 143.

25. Temby, "Imagining," 33; Solahudin, *Roots*, 150.

26. Sulastri Osman, "Jemaah Islamiyah: Of Kin and Kind," *Journal of Current Southeast Asian Affairs* 39:2 (2010): 8; Sidney Jones, "Inherited Jihadism: Like Father, Like Son," *Australian Financial Review*, July 4, 2007.

27. Ibid., 9.

28. Ibid.

29. Sidney Jones, "The Changing Nature of Jemaah Islamiyah," *Australian Journal of International Affairs* 59:2 (2005): 170.

30. There was also the fourth or the "other" Mantiqi (Mantiqi Ukhro), comprising Papua and Australia. It was designated as a supporting economic area, but very little in the way of activity ever took place there.

31. Markaziyah of Jemaah Islamiyah, "The General Guidelines of Struggle of Jemaah Islamiyah," 1996, 5.

32. Elena Pavlova, "Jemaah Islamiyah according to the PUPJI," in *A Handbook of Terrorism and Insurgency in Southeast Asia*, ed. Andrew T. H. Tan (Cheltenham, UK: Edward Elgar, 2007), 82.

33. Ibid., 84.

34. Markaziyah of Jemaah Islamiyah, "The General Guidelines of Struggle of Jemaah Islamiyah," 30.

35. Greg Fealy, "Militant Java-Based Islamist Movements," in Tan, *Handbook*, 72.

36. Ibid.

37. Solahudin, *Roots*, 161.

38. Ibid., 163–64.

39. Ibid.

40. Julie Chernov Hwang, "Terrorism in Perspective: An Assessment of 'Jihad Project' Trends in Indonesia," *Asia Pacific Issues*, no. 104 (September 2012): 3.

41. Solahudin, *Roots*, 172.

42. Pavlova, "Jemaah Islamiyah," 77.

43. Solahudin, *Roots*, 172.

44. Jones, "Changing Nature," 173.

45. Ibid.

46. Nasir Abas, interview with the author, March 2006, Jakarta, Indonesia.

47. Solahudin, *Roots*, 181.

48. Ibid.

49. Pavlova, "Jemaah Islamiyah," 77.

50. Chernov Hwang, "Terrorism in Perspective," 3.

51. Julie Chernov Hwang, Rizal Panggabean, and Ihsan Ali Fauzi, "When We Were Separated, We Began to Think for Ourselves Again: The Disengagement of Jihadis in Poso, Indonesia," *Asian Survey* 53:4 (2013): 761.

52. Idul Fitri is the feast holiday marking the end of Ramadan.

53. Dave McRae, *A Few Poorly Organized Men: Interreligious Violence in Poso, Indonesia* (Sydney: Brill, 2013), 96.

54. These conflicts broke out several months after the police were separated from the military. Thus, both forces faced a learning curve with regard to their new roles and conflict over turf. This hindered the ability of either force to effectively respond to the initial outbreak of violence. Van Klinken also notes that resources in Maluku were exceedingly thin. In March 1999, two months after the first outbreak of violence, there were only fifty-three hundred combined military and police forces in a territory spread out over hundreds of islands and a population of two million people; by November, the number of police had increased by only seven hundred. Gerry Van Klinken, "Maluku Wars: Bringing Society Back In," *Indonesia* 71 (2001): 3.

55. Ibid.

56. Solahudin, *Roots*, 193.

57. Chernov Hwang, Panggabean, and Fauzi, "When We Were Separated," 761.

58. Nasir Abas, interview with the author, January 2012, Jakarta, Indonesia.

59. Ibid.

60. Sidney Jones, "The Fall and Rise of Jemaah Islamiyah," in *Indonesian Terrorism*, ed. Greg Fealy and Sally White (London: Routledge, forthcoming), 2.

61. Chernov Hwang, Panggabean, and Fauzi, "When We Were Separated," 763.

62. Dave McRae, "Reintegration and Localized Conflict: Security Impacts beyond Influencing Spoilers," *Conflict, Security and Development* 10:3 (2010): 408.

63. Solahudin, *Roots*, 195.

64. Ibid.

65. Ibid., 190.

66. Ibid., 195.

67. International Crisis Group, *Terrorism in Indonesia: Noordin's Networks*, Asia Report no. 114, May 5, 2006, 1.

68. Jones, "Changing Nature."

69. Sidney Jones, "The Changing Threat of Terrorism in Indonesia," speech at the Asia Strategic Policy Institute, September 15, 2005.

70. Jones, "Changing Nature," 170.

71. E-mail correspondence with Sidney Jones.

72. Sidney Jones, "Poso's Jihadist Network," *Jane's Terrorism and Insurgency Monitor*, February 2013, 16.

73. Sidney Jones, "Whatever Happened to JI?," paper presented at Indonesian Terrorism in a Global Context conference, Australian National University, December 5, 2011, 4.

74. International Crisis Group, *Jihadi Surprise in Aceh*, Asia Report no. 189, April 20, 2010, 7.

75. Ibid., 16, 7, 12.

76. Jones, "Whatever Happened to JI?," 10–12.

77. "Jemaah Islamiyah Active Again in Indonesia, Recruiting and Collecting Funds," Reuters, February 15, 2016.

78. Jones, "Whatever Happened to JI?," 10.

79. "End of the Year Report 2013 Tarbiyah Directorate," PowerPoint from Jemaah Islamiyah's Tarbiyah directorate, passed along by Kirsten Schulze.

80. Ibid.

81. Jones, "Whatever Happened to JI?," 10.

82. Ibid., 11.

83. Ibid.

84. Institute for Policy Analysis of Conflict, *Indonesians and the Syrian Conflict*, Report no. 6, January 2014, 10–11.

85. Ibid.

2. Patterns of Disengagement

1. Phrase used in Tore Bjørgo, "The Process of Disengagement from Violent Groups of the Extreme Right," in *Leaving Terrorism Behind: Individual and Collective Disengagement*, ed. John Horgan and Tore Bjørgo (London: Routledge, 2009), 37.

2. Former member of JI and Afghan veteran, interview with the author, July 2010, Jakarta, Indonesia.

3. These are just a sampling of the criticisms of various JI and KOMPAK leaders, usually someone's direct senior. These interviews were conducted in June 2011 in Jakarta, Semarang, and Surabaya.

4. These are a sampling of criticisms specifically pertaining to Ustad Abu Bakar Ba'asyir. They were made by various individuals in Jakarta and Poso in July 2010 and June 2011.

5. Ibid.

6. Ibid.

7. Former JI member and Afghan veteran, interview with the author, January 2012, Jakarta, Indonesia.

8. Muhammadiyah is an Indonesian Islamic mass organization with a membership close to thirty million.

9. Former KOMPAK operative, interview with the author, June 2011, Jakarta, Indonesia.

10. Amir, former member of KOMPAK, interview with the author, January 2012, Surabaya, Indonesia.

11. Ali Fauzi, interview with the author, July 2011, Surabaya, Indonesia.

12. JI member and Afghan veteran, interview with the author, January 2012, Jakarta, Indonesia.

13. One former member of KOMPAK and one former member (founding member) of JI, interviews with the author, June 2011, Jakarta, Indonesia.

14. Sam, a current member of Ring Banten, interview with the author, January 2012, Banten, Indonesia.

15. Ibid.

16. Institute for Policy Analysis of Conflict, *Countering Violent Extremism in Indonesia: Need for a Rethink*, Report no. 11, June 20, 2014, 9, 15.

17. Former Ambon fighter, interview with the author, January 2012, Surabaya, Indonesia.

18. Afghan veteran, interview with the author, July 2010, Jakarta, Indonesia.

19. Member of Subur cell, interview with the author, January 2012, Semarang, Indonesia.

20. Ibid.

21. Sidney Jones, "After Abu Dujana and Nuaim," *Tempo*, June 19, 2007.

22. "Amru," former JI member, interview with the author, June 2011, Semarang, Indonesia.

23. Ibid.

24. Former member of Tanah Runtuh (from the first generation of recruits), interview with the author, June 2011, Palu, Indonesia.

25. Former member of elite-level *askari 3*, Tanah Runtuh, interview with the author, Palu, Indonesia, July 2010.

26. Former Ambon fighter, interview with the author, January 2012, Surabaya, Indonesia.

27. Ali Fauzi and Noor Huda Ismail, interviews with the author, July 2011, Surabaya, Indonesia.

28. Former member of JI and current Salafi, interview with the author, January 2012, Jakarta, Indonesia.

29. Tanah Runtuh member (from the first generation of recruits), interview with the author, January 2012, Jakarta, Indonesia.

30. "Laporan Kegiatan Badan Reserse Kriminal POLRI Detasemen Khusus 88 Anti-Teror Asep Djaja" [Report by Densus 88 on Asep Djaja], 2.

31. Institute for Policy Analysis of Conflict, *ISIS in Ambon*, no. 28, May 13, 2016, 4.

32. "Anas," a former operative from KOMPAK, interview with the author, January 2012, Jakarta, Indonesia.

33. Abdul Rauf, late member of Ring Banten and ISIS, interview with the author, January 2012, Banten, Indonesia.

34. Former member of KOMPAK, interview with the author, June 2011, Jakarta, Indonesia.

35. Member of the *ikwan awal* (original generation/first generation) of Tanah Runtuh, interview with the author, July 2011, Palu, Indonesia.

36. Ibid.

3. Anas

1. Tarbiyah would go on to form the Justice Party (PK) in 1998, following the fall of the Suharto dictatorship, and the Prosperous Justice Party (PKS) in 2003, following a poor showing in the 1999 elections.

4. B.R.

1. Dave McRae, *A Few Poorly Organized Men: Interreligious Violence in Poso, Indonesia* (Sydney: Brill, 2013), 60–61.

2. Ibid., 65–66, 68.

3. Ibid., 75, 88, 89.

4. A.B. wrote regularly to let her know that B.R. was safe, but she never disclosed that he was living with them in Palu.

5. Ali Imron

1. Sally Neighbour, *In the Shadow of Swords: How Islamic Terrorists Declared War on Australia* (Sidney: HarperCollins, 2004), 34–35.
2. Ali Imron cited strict regulations to me in an interview. He cites "extreme lessons" to Sally Neighbour in *In the Shadow of Swords*, 61.
3. Ali Imron, *Ali Imron Sang Pengebom* [Ali Imron, the bomber] (Jakarta: Republika, 2007), 4.
4. Ibid.
5. Ibid., 4–5.

7. Yuda

1. International Crisis Group, *Jihadism in Indonesia: Poso on the Edge*, Asia Report no. 127, January 24, 2007, 5.
2. M. Tito Karnavian, *Indonesian Top Secret: Membongkar Konflik Poso* [Uncovering the Poso conflict] (Jakarta: Gramaedia, 2008), 293–310.
3. This was confirmed by sources both within Tanah Runtuh and outside it.

8. The Role of the State and Civil Society in Disengagement Initiatives

1. Ali Imron, *Ali Imron Sang Pengebom* [Ali Imron, the bomber] (Jakarta: Republika, 2007).
2. International Crisis Group, *"Deradicalisation" and Indonesian Prisons*, Asia Report no. 142, November 19, 2007, 12.
3. Ibid., 13.
4. Zachary Abuza, "The Rehabilitation of Jemaah Islamiyah Detainees," in *Leaving Terrorism Behind: Individual and Collective Disengagement*, ed. John Horgan and Tore Bjørgo (London: Routledge, 2009), 200.
5. These outings were cited by a handful of interviewees who served time at POLDA Metro.
6. Tito Karnavian, "Terrorist Rehabilitation: Indonesia's Experience," paper presented at the International Center for Political Violence and Terrorism Research Conference, Singapore, February 24–26, 2009, 36.
7. Member of the hit squad Tanah Runtuh, interview with the author, Palu Prison, July 2010, Palu, Indonesia.
8. Karnavian, "Terrorist Rehabilitation," 36.
9. Tito Karnavian, interview with the author, July 2010, Jakarta, Indonesia.
10. Tito Karnavian, "The Soft Approach Strategy in Coping with Islamist Terrorism in Indonesia," working paper, n.p., 15.
11. International Crisis Group, *"Deradicalisation" and Indonesian Prisons*, 14.
12. Julie Chernov Hwang, "Terrorism in Perspective: An Assessment of 'Jihad Project' Trends in Indonesia," *Asia-Pacific Issues*, no. 104 (September 2012): 10.

13. Ibid.

14. Ampana fighter, interview with the author, January 2012, Ampana, Indonesia.

15. Former member of Subur cell, interview with the author, January 2012, Semarang, Indonesia.

16. Viola Gienger, "Use of Terrorist 'Dropouts' to Boost Defections: Dangerous Business," United States Institute of Peace, May 1, 2013, http://www.usip.org/publications/use-of-terrorist-dropouts-boost-defections-dangerous-business.

17. Ibid.

18. Julie Chernov Hwang, Rizal Panggabean, and Ihsan Ali Fauzi, "When We Were Separated, We Began to Think for Ourselves Again: The Disengagement of Indonesian Jihadists in Poso, Indonesia," *Asian Survey* 53:4 (2013).

19. Ibid.

20. Ibid.

21. Head of National Unity and Community Protection Agency, interview with the author, July 2010, Poso, Indonesia.

22. Former member of Tanah Runtuh, interview with the author, July 2010, Poso, Indonesia.

23. Dave McRae, "Reintegration and Localized Conflict: Security Impacts beyond Influencing Spoilers," *Conflict, Security and Development* 10:3 (2010): 413–15.

24. Institute for Policy Analysis of Conflict, *Countering Violent Extremism: Need for a Rethink*, Report no. 11, June 20, 2014, 1.

25. Ibid., 2.

26. Ibid., 3.

27. Ibid, 4.

28. Agus Hadi Nahrowi, program manager, Search for Common Ground; Zora Sukabdi, executive director, INSEP; and Taufik Andrie, executive director, Institute for International Peace Building, interviews with the author, July 2014, Jakarta, Indonesia.

29. Zora Sukabdi, executive director, INSEP, interview with the author, July 2014, Jakarta, Indonesia.

30. Nahrowi, Sukabdi, and Andrie, interviews, July 2014.

31. Ibid.

32. Taufik Andrie, executive director of the Institute for International Peace Building, interview with the author, July 2014, Jakarta, Indonesia.

33. Institute for Policy Analysis of Conflict, *Countering Violent Extremism*, 8.

34. Ibid.

35. Sidney Jones, "The Fall and Rise of Jemaah Islamiyah," in *Indonesian Terrorism*, ed. Greg Fealy and Sally White (London: Routledge, forthcoming), 22.

36. Ibid., 15.

37. Institute for Policy Analysis of Conflict, *Update on Indonesian Pro-ISIS Prisoners and Deradicalization Efforts*, December 14, 2016, 1.

38. Ibid., 51.

39. Institute for Policy Analysis of Conflict, *Prison Problems: Planned and Unplanned Releases of Convicted Extremists in Indonesia*, Report no. 2, September 2, 2013, 1.

40. Ibid.

41. Institute for Policy Analysis of Conflict, *Update on Indonesian Pro-ISIS Prisoners*.

42. Institute for Policy Analysis of Conflict, *Indonesia's Lamongan Network: How Java, Poso and Syria are Linked*, Report no. 18, April 15, 2015, 17–18.

43. Ibid., 18.

44. Ibid.

45. Sukabdi interview, July 2014.

46. Agus Nahrowi, program manager, Search for Common Ground, interview with the author, July 2014, Jakarta, Indonesia.

47. Ibid.

48. Andrie interview, July 2014.

49. Ibid.

50. Ibid.

51. Noor Huda Ismail, former executive director of the Institute for International Peace Building, interview with the author, July 2012, Semarang, Indonesia.

52. Yusuf Adhirama, manager, Dapur Bistek, interview with the author, June 2012, Semarang, Indonesia.

53. Andrie interview, July 2014.

54. Sarlito Sarwono, former dean of the psychology faculty at the University of Indonesia, interview with the author, July 2014, Jakarta, Indonesia.

55. Mark Woodward, Ali Amin, and Inayah Rohmaniyah, *Lessons from Aceh Terrorist De-radicalization*, Consortium for Strategic Communication, Arizona State University, Report no. 1001, May 13, 2010, 7.

56. Jones, "Rise and Fall," 22.

57. Institute for Policy Analysis of Conflict, *Update on Indonesian Pro-ISIS Prisoners*, 5.

58. Ibid., 22.

59. Ibid.

60. Anas, interview with the author, June 2015, at his home, Bogor, Indonesia.

61. Taufik Andrie, executive director of the Institute for International Peace Building, interview with the author, June 2015, Jakarta, Indonesia.

62. Anas interview, June 2015.

63. "Penguatan Pendidikan Karakter Toleransi dan Anti Kekerasan" [Strengthening character education, tolerance, and anti-violence], Maarif Institute for Culture and Humanity, PowerPoint, 2015.

64. Ibid.
65. Ibid.
66. Ibid.
67. Ibid.

Conclusion

1. Fendina Sundaryani, "IS Is Not Worth Joining: Returnee," *Jakarta Post*, April 1, 2015.

2. Ibid.

3. Fendina Sundaryani, "The Trip Home from Syria Was Easy," *Jakarta Post*, April 2, 2015.

4. Institute for Policy Analysis of Conflict, *Countering Violent Extremism in Indonesia*, Report no. 11, June 30, 2014, 3.

5. John Horgan, "What Makes a Terrorist Stop Being a Terrorist?," *Journal for Deradicalization*, Winter 2014/2015: 3.

6. Ibid.

7. Marieke Denissen, "Reintegrating Ex-combatants into Civilian Life," *Peace and Change* 35:2 (April 2010): 338.

8. Anne Speckhard and Ahmet Yayla, "Eyewitness Accounts from Recent Defectors from the Islamic State: Why They Joined, What They Saw, Why They Quit," *Perspectives on Terrorism* 9:6 (2015).

9. Ibid.

10. Peter R. Neumann, *Victims, Perpetrators, Assets: The Narratives of Islamic State Defectors*, International Center for the Study of Radicalization and Political Violence, 2015, 10–11.

11. Ibid.

12. Omar Ashour, "Islamist Deradicalization in Algeria: Successes and Failures," Middle East Institute Policy Brief, no. 21, November 2008, 8–9.

13. Fernando Reinares, "Exit from Terrorism: A Qualitative Empirical Study on Disengagement and Deradicalization among Members of ETA," *Terrorism and Political Violence* 23:5 (2011): 780; Tore Bjørgo, "The Process of Disengagement from Violent Groups of the Extreme Right," in *Leaving Terrorism Behind: Individual and Collective Disengagement*, ed. John Horgan and Tore Bjørgo (London: Routledge, 2009), 39–40; John Horgan, *Walking Away from Terrorism: Accounts of Disengagement from Radical and Extremist Movements* (London: Routledge, 2009), 59.

14. Marybeth Altier, Christian Thoroughgood, and John Horgan, "Turning Away from Terrorism: Lessons from Psychology, Sociology, and Criminology," *Journal of Peace Research* 51:5 (2014): 649; Bjørgo, "Process of Disengagement," 39–40; Reinares, "Exit," 780.

Glossary

adab al-jihad—The rules/norms of war.

al Mukmim (also **Ngruki**; also **al Mu'mim**)—The boarding school established by Abu Bakar Ba'asyir and Abdullah Sungkar. Several of the Bali bombers had attended or taught at al Mukmim.

amir—Emir; the head of a network/movement.

amaliyah—Actions. Used by Indonesian jihadists to refer to terrorist attacks.

dai—Preachers.

dakwah—Islamic propagation and proselytizing activities.

fai—Robbing "unbelievers" to pay for jihad activities.

fard al kifaya—A collective obligation. Used to refer to jihad as a collective obligation. Requires a leader to sanction it.

fardu ain—Individual obligation for jihad that is incumbent on each and every able-bodied Muslim.

fiqh jihad—The religious laws governing the proper conduct of jihad.

i'dad—Preparations (for jihad). This could be training or gathering weapons, resources, or materials.

ikhwan—Brothers. This is the term the jihadists use for one another.

jihad—There are two kinds of jihad: the greater jihad and the lesser jihad. The greater jihad is the struggle against one's baser instincts. The lesser jihad is *jihad qital* or holy war.

jihad difaa'i—Defensive jihad.

kafir—A term of slander implying an infidel or an apostate from Islam.

Laskar Khos—The paramilitary wing of Jemaah Islamiyah. Zulkarnaen was the first head of the Laskar Khos.

Luqmanul Hakim—An Islamic boarding school in Malaysia that became the hub for JI's pro-bombing wing.

madrasa—Islamic day school.

Ma'had Ali—Postsecondary education within an Islamic boarding school.

Mantiqi—The name given to the original geographic divisions within Jemaah Islamiyah. Mantiqi 1, comprising Malaysia and Singapore, was the fund-raising region. Mantiqi 2, the recruitment region, was made up of large portions of Indonesia. Between 1993 and 1997, JI had only these two Mantiqis. In 1997, it added Mantiqi 3, the training region, comprising the state of Sabah in East Malaysia, the Southern Philippines, and Kalimantan, Ambon, and Central Sulawesi in Indonesia. There was also a fourth Mantiqi, made up of Australia and Papua that was designated as a supporting economic area. Below the Mantiqis, the structure resembled that of a military organization with brigades, companies, platoons, and squads. Arrests in Malaysia and Indonesia in 2001 and 2002 decimated Mantiqi 1. By 2005, the Mantiqi structure had been entirely abandoned in favor of a new structure centered on Indonesia with a far smaller paramilitary wing.

Markaziyah—The central command or central board of Jemaah Islamiyah in its early iteration.

muhasabah—The Correct Path.

pengajian—Teachings/lecture.

pesantren—Islamic boarding school.

qital—Battle or war (*jihad qital*).

qoidul aminah—A secure base. This concept first appeared with Darul Islam. It features prominently in the General Guidelines of Struggle of Jemaah Islamiyah (PUPJI). JI's most successful attempt to implement a secure base was between 2001 and 2006 in Poso.

sami'na wa atho'na—I hear and I obey. This is the logic given why one would obey an order he personally found morally wrong—he would feel bound by *sami'na wa atho'na*.

sholat—Prayer.

syahid—Martyr.

takfir—The practice of declaring Muslims who don't agree with you as *kafir*, thus legitimating their murder. This practice is largely discouraged within the Indonesian jihadist community.

taklim—Religious study groups.

tanzim siri—Clandestine/underground organization.

tarbiyah—Islamic education.

tauhid—The divine oneness of God.

usroh—Cell. Used to refer to small Islamist study circles.

ustad—Teacher.

Index

Abas, Nasir, 35, 41, 69, 103–104, 109,
    141–146, 166, 178
Abdurrahman, Aman, 46, 85, 89, 169
Aceh, 23, 31, 44, 59, 159
Al Chairat, 19, 48,
Al Gamaah al Islamiyah, 2, 183
Al Qaeda in the Malay Archipelago, 14, 42
alternative social network, 8–9, 56, 62,
    73, 75, 78, 105, 155, 173–177
  business, 59–60, 159
  family, 8, 9, 11, 50, 57, 60–63, 71, 77,
    78, 102, 105, 164, 176–177
  friends, 7, 57–58, 62–63, 86–87,
    98–101, 130, 132, 173–175
amaliyah, 44
Ambon, 1, 14, 19, 36, 40, 75, 82, 89, 111, 113
Ambon conflict, 14, 19, 36, 37, 40–41,
    55, 61, 65–74, 78, 80–81, 91–92,
    110–113, 118, 120, 124–128, 131, 154
  bloody Idul Fitri, 37, 110
  Loki attack, 66–68, 153, 174
Amrozi, 41, 62, 111–117, 121, 125, 128, 129
Andrie, Taufik, 69, 158, 159, 163
Arsal, Haji Adnan, 38, 63, 93, 99–100, 103
Azzam, Abdullah, 53, 80

Ba'asyir, Abu Bakar, 14, 18, 25, 27, 31,
    35, 43, 51–52, 106, 112, 117
Bjorgo, Tore, 11

cost-benefit analysis, 8, 55, 58, 63–64, 70,
    77–78, 87, 90, 116, 151, 168, 170,
    172–173, 183
  context, 8, 12, 54, 95, 139, 172
counter-radicalization, 149, 151, 164, 165

dakwah, 32, 33, 36, 39, 44, 55, 56, 58, 61,
    64, 118
Dapur Bistek, 159–160, 175
Darul Islam, 14, 16, 17, 18, 23–30
  kinship, 18, 30
  origin, 23–24
  Qoidul Aminah, 30
  recruitment, 24–27
  Ring Banten, 18, 31, 43–44, 59, 72
  split with JI, 29–30
Densus 88, 1, 40, 43–44, 85, 88, 100, 103,
    136, 137, 140–145, 149, 152, 163
  soft approach, 141, 143–147, 166
Department of Corrections (DGC), 141,
    149, 153, 157, 160
deradicalization, 4, 10, 12, 131, 140, 147,
    149–150, 152–154, 178–180
  Danish program, 13, 168, 180
  Sabaoon, 168, 180
  Saudi Program, 12–13
  Singaporean program, 12–13
Dewan Dakwah Islamiyah Indonesia
    (DDII), 25, 37, 64–65

disengagement, 3–13, 21, 30, 48, 49–51, 53–55, 57–61, 63, 65, 67, 68, 69, 77, 78, 87, 90, 101–105, 120, 129, 132, 140, 145–147, 149–160, 164–165, 168, 170, 171–184
  conditionality, 7, 71–72, 78, 104
disillusionment, 5, 8, 9, 11, 12, 51–54, 56, 63, 69–70, 72, 77, 78, 168, 171–173
  tactics, 8, 50, 52, 114, 116, 120, 170
  leaders, 8, 51–52, 117, 120
  seniors, 87, 89, 90
Dulmatin, 41, 44, 74, 82, 88, 111, 127

East Indonesia Holy Warriors (MIT), 44–46, 61, 63, 75–77, 104, 139, 148, 170, 172

fa'i, 25, 30
Fauzi, Ali, 55, 62, 66, 109–110, 117–118, 120–130, 139, 159, 164, 166, 169, 173–174
  mutual aid society, 120, 131–132, 154–155, 161–162, 175

Gufron, Ali. See *Muchlas*

Hambali, 29, 34–36, 39, 40, 42, 51–53, 111, 116–117, 124
Hasanuddin, 39, 95, 135
Hilal Ahmar Society Indonesia (HASI), 46
Horgan, John, 11–12
Husin, Azhari, 17, 42, 43

i'dad, 44
Indonesian Institute for Societal Empowerment (INSEP), 156, 157, 161, 162, 164, 179
Institute for International Peacebuilding (YPP), 156, 158–162, 179
Islamic Defenders Front (FPI), 35
Islamic State of Iraq and Syria (ISIS), 10, 13, 15, 18, 21, 46, 47, 72, 76, 131, 154–155, 167–168, 179–180, 182–183
Islamic Youth Movement (GPI), 25
Ismail, Noor Huda, 62–63, 69, 128–129, 158–159, 175

Jabhat Fateh el Shams, 46–47
Jemaah Anshorut Tauhid (JAT), 31, 44–46, 148
Jemaah Islamiyah (JI), 1, 4, 6, 7, 14–16, 22–23, 25, 29–41, 44–47, 59, 69, 77, 80–82, 86, 93, 95, 103, 110, 141, 145, 170, 172–173
  Laskar Khos, 110–111
  Majlis Dakwah Ummat Islam (MDUI) 46
  mantiqis, 31–35, 39, 41, 51–52, 69, 103, 109, 141
  Markaziyah, 117
  organizational structure, 31–33
  Osama Bin laden Fatwa, 33–35, 53–54, 111, 126, 142
  Project Uhud, 39, 43
  PUPJI, 31, 32, 39
  split with Darul Islam, 29–30
  tanzim siri, 32
Jemaah Islamiyah schools, 18
  Al Islam, 109–111, 126, 132, 155
  Luqmanul Hakim, 122, 123, 124, 126–127, 130
  Ngruki, 18, 19, 27, 28, 106, 112, 121
  Al Mukmim. See *Jemaah Islamiyah schools: Ngruki*
jihad, 7, 17, 24–25, 32, 34, 36–38, 40, 46, 47, 52–53, 55–57, 60–62, 66–67, 69, 74, 76, 78, 80–82, 87, 89, 92–93, 95, 107, 109–113, 114–119, 122–124, 126–128, 132, 135, 142, 173–174
  defensive jihad, 29, 72, 78, 125,
  fard al-ain, 29
  fard al-kifaya, 28
  fiqh jihad, 109, 118, 123, 134
  jihadi-Salafi, 12, 18, 28, 29
  jihad qital, 16, 19, 20, 27, 28, 36, 49, 71, 76, 120, 124, 173
  lust for jihad, 87
  post-jihad identity, 9, 50, 64, 77, 147, 165, 174
Jones, Sidney, 13, 18, 30, 34, 43, 162

Kalla, Yusuf, 94
Karnavian, Tito, 141, 143–145
Kartosuwirjo, Sekarmadji Maridjan, 23, 28, 107, 122
Komite Aksi Penanggulangan Akibat Krisis (KOMPAK), 37, 64–65

Lamongan, 109, 112, 120, 126, 131, 154, 155, 180
Laskar Jihad, 3, 15, 91–93
  Ahl Sunna Communication Forum (FKAWJ), 3
Laskar Jundullah, 14
Lintas Tanzim, 44, 159

Malaysia, 4, 12, 27, 31–33, 35, 42–43, 52, 107, 112, 122, 124, 126, 141
Masduki, Ajengan, 17, 30
Masyumi, 24, 25
Mindanao, 17, 31, 33–34, 39, 4, 55, 59, 93, 111, 124, 131, 142, 159
  Camp Abu Bakar, 32, 124
  Camp Hudaibiyah, 31–33, 55, 135, 142
  Moro conflicts, 19, 123, 154
  Moro Islamic Liberation Front (MILF), 29, 34, 39, 66, 124, 126, 127
Ministry of Law and Human Rights (BAPAS), 162, 181
Muchlas, 34, 41–42, 62, 80, 82, 88, 106–109, 111–112, 114–117, 121–124, 126–129, 154, 171
Muhammadiyah, 6, 19, 25, 35, 48, 54, 61–62, 73, 75–76, 107, 121, 129–132, 159, 175
Mujahidin Kayamanya, 14–16, 38, 47
Mujahidin KOMPAK, 14–16, 31, 37–38, 43–44, 47, 54–56, 59, 64, 66, 73–74, 77, 81, 83, 93, 110, 125, 131–132, 153, 155, 172
  origins, 37, 64, 110
  relationship to JI, 37, 110
  Waimorat training, 37, 110
  Ma'arif Institute, 164–165

Mujahidin Indonesia Timor (MIT).
  See *East Indonesia Holy Warriors*
Munandar, Aris, 64–65, 81, 84, 110, 125

Nahdlatul Ulama, 6, 24, 35, 48, 54
National Counter Terrorism Bureau (BNPT), 141, 148–150, 152, 153, 160–162, 165–166, 177–178, 180

Pancasila, 23, 26, 178, 189
  azas tunggal, 26
Patek, Umar, 41, 74, 127
pengajian, 17, 45
pesantren, 18, 121
Porong Prison, 70, 153, 154, 157, 161, 163, 179
  Asep Jaja, 153, 161
Poso, 14–16, 19, 31, 35–41, 43–45, 53–55, 57–59, 62, 66, 71–72, 74–75, 78, 88, 91–93, 95–102, 104–105, 111, 113, 120, 125–128, 131, 133–136, 138, 146–148, 154–155, 160, 163, 170, 172, 174–175, 180
Poso conflict
  JI arrival, 16, 30, 38–39
  Malino Peace Accords, 94, 135
  Walisongo, 16, 37–38, 92–94, 125, 134–135
Priority Shifts, 9, 12, 61–62, 64, 140, 174, 175, 182–183
Prosperous Justice Party (PKS), 84–86
  Justice Party (PK), 80, 107
  KAMMI, 107
  Tarbiyah movement, 49, 79, 80, 84, 107

Qutb, Syed, 24, 80

Rauf, Abdul, 18, 72
reintegration, 7–9, 12–13, 47, 50, 56–57, 62, 75, 77, 131–132, 140–141, 145, 147–148, 154–156, 160, 163–164, 166, 168, 170, 173–175, 177–183
Rusdan, Abu, 34, 41, 46, 56

sami'na wa atho 'na, 53, 54, 74, 172
Samudra, Imam, 28, 42, 52, 82, 111–112, 114–116, 128, 129
Sarwono, Sarlito, 147, 156, 160–161
Search for Common Ground, 69, 156–157, 161–162
Singapore, 4, 12–13, 31, 33, 43, 108, 112, 145, 147
Solahudin, 28, 35
Southern Philippines, 19, 31, 33, 41
Soviet-Afghan War, 16, 19, 20, 22, 27, 29, 51, 71, 107, 109, 131, 142, 170
    Afghan veterans, 14, 20, 29, 35, 49, 55, 56, 71–72, 145, 155, 179
    As Sadaah, 27, 142
    ideology, 28–29
    Indonesian recruits, 27–28
    training, 28–29
Subur Cell, 15, 17, 58, 146
Suharto, 23, 24, 26, 27, 35, 37, 64, 80
Sukabdi, Zora, 157
Sunata, Abdullah, 64, 73–75, 83, 176
Sungkar, Abdullah, 14, 18, 25, 27, 29, 30, 52, 106, 108, 120, 123
Suryadharma, 1, 2, 85, 86, 90, 141, 143, 174, 176, 177

Takfir, 2, 85, 87, 151, 169, 178–179, 185
Taklim, 16, 66, 122, 134
Tanah Runtuh, 14–16, 21, 38–40, 44–45, 47, 60–63, 72, 93–100, 102–105, 135–137, 139, 143–144, 148, 167–169, 170, 172–174, 184
    2007 Raids, 43, 60, 176,
    hit squad, 39, 61, 95, 138, 143,
    mutilation of the schoolgirls, 99, 136, 139
    relationship to JI, 30, 36, 38, 39, 93, 135

team of 10, 63, 94, 95
Tentena market bombing, 39, 60, 97
tarbiyah, 32, 36
tauhid, 17, 24, 130, 164
Tauhid wa'al Jihad, 15
Tentara Nasional Indonesia (TNI), 114
terrorist attacks, 14–15, 19–20, 35, 40, 44, 120, 131, 145
    Atrium Mall bombing, 14, 20, 35, 111, 113, 118
    Australian Embassy bombing, 42, 74, 75, 83
    Bali Bombing I, 1, 3, 14, 17, 20, 22, 28, 32, 33, 35, 41, 43, 45, 56, 74, 80, 82, 95, 111, 113–117, 119, 126–128, 141, 142, 146, 152, 154, 169, 171
    Bali Bombing II, 17, 42
    Christmas Eve bombing, 20, 35, 87, 111, 113, 119, 142
    JW Marriott bombing, 14, 87
    Kunningan bombing. See *terrorist attacks: Australian Embassy Bombing*
    Marriot and Ritz Carlton bombing, 42, 87, 149
    Philippine Ambassador's Residence bombing, 1, 20, 57, 87, 111, 118, 142
Tholut, Abu, 39, 41, 59
Top, Noordin, 17, 42–44

United Development Party, 23, 26
usroh, 26–28

Yudhoyono, Susilo Bambang, 94

Zarkasih, 40, 56
Zulkarnaen, 81, 108, 110–111, 124

CPSIA information can be obtained
at www.ICGtesting.com
Printed in the USA
BVOW06*1451060218
507349BV00001B/11/P